For Here or To Go?

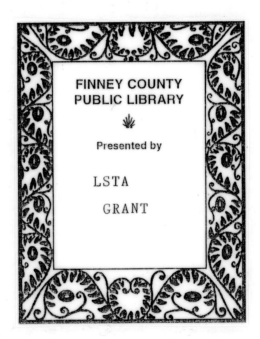

For Here or To Go?

John de Szendeffy

Ann Arbor

THE UNIVERSITY OF MICHIGAN PRESS

Copyright © by the University of Michigan 1997
All rights reserved
ISBN 0-472-08397-X
Library of Congress Catalog Card No. 97-60204
Published in the United States of America by
The University of Michigan Press
Manufactured in the United States of America

♾ Printed on acid-free paper

2004   2003   2002   2001   6   5   4   3

To my most devout fair and foul weather fan, Linda D'Amore, my wife and the best friend I've ever had. And to my mother, Mildred. (Need I say more? She's my mother.)

Preface

I wrote this text because I couldn't find one like it to use in class. The anecdotal quality of its readings and the content of those readings (student perspectives on adjusting to a new culture) fill what I see as a relative void in English as a second language (ESL) reading texts. It is the second language reader that I, as a student, would want.

For Here or To Go? is a collection of readings and activities for ESL students, one designed to supplement comprehensive instruction or provide accessible material for self-study. The readings, all written in the first person, are composite stories based on the experiences of ESL students from a variety of home countries (Japan, Vietnam, Iran, Russia, the Dominican Republic, Venezuela, Saudi Arabia, Argentina, China, France, Korea, and Kenya). The stories, which range in length from 470 to 1,360 words, revolve around the themes of confronting a new language and acclimating to a new home—themes with which ESL students easily identify. Some stories are lighthearted whereas others border on tragic; in any case, they represent *real* experiences.

How did these stories come about? Among my own ESL students in Boston, I have found that use of relevant anecdotal material stimulates lively discussion and student identification with the topics. Such reaction to these anecdotes convinced me of their value as intensely personal and stimulating content. Although some of the stories in *For Here or To Go?* may seem to reinforce stereotypes about the adjustment difficulties of ESL students, all are based on actual incidents. This simplified approach to the complex issues involved in adapting to a new culture will prepare students for later, more sophisticated inquiry into the same subjects.

Purpose

A beginning-level second language reader should acquaint students with the language of elementary discourse. The readings should provide models of native fluency, demonstrating the vocabulary, structure, mechanics, and rhetorical patterns of English. Some ESL texts at this level have also included cultural instruction, becoming, in effect, primers on U.S. culture. The problem with this approach is that it may be pedagogically less efficient in that students may acquire the cultural data at the expense of linguistic achievement, attempting to interpret an unfamiliar culture with unfamiliar tools.

For Here or To Go? deals only incidentally with specific cultural information. In general, the stories and exercises focus on *universals* of human experience and on language as used in context, providing models of native fluency that interest students because they are authentic (in origin) and mature stories written in simple prose. After all, students will begin to truly understand a new culture only after acquiring the linguistic tools to explore it firsthand.

Benefits of This Approach

The stories in *For Here or To Go?* involve situations and perspectives either familiar to or easily imagined by students and therefore will engage students' interest and provoke discussion. Recent arrivals to a new country (the United States in this case) want to learn about their new cultural and linguistic environment, but they also need to be reassured that they have certain experiences in common with other adults or young adults transplanted to a new country, a new life. *Disagreement* with the viewpoint presented in a story provides students with added impetus to engage in discussion or other response activities.

Because this is a beginning-level second language text, I have avoided the use of grammar and structures more typical of advanced-level texts or authentic materials. However, I have *not* tightly controlled language to present specific grammatical emphases, because this tends to result in the sort of contrived, nonnative writing that intelligent readers see through and lose interest in. Therefore, no overt grammar instruction is presented (other than the derived forms tables at the ends of the chapters). I have tried to avoid the paradox of trying to teach too many things at once and none of them well.

This text also assumes that to acquire language successfully, students must have significant exposure to the target language. The length and accessibility of the readings invite students to immerse themselves in a story, one with which they may personally identify, before shifting their focus to exercises and activities.

Level

For Here or To Go? assumes student familiarity with a high-beginning to low-intermediate-level ESL grammar repertoire (e.g., past and perfect tenses, conjunctions, appositives, adjective clauses) and a readiness to work with elementary discourse. Passive, conditional, and complex dependent structures have been avoided. Reported speech is used only in the last chapters. The stories and exercises progress in form, however, to the high-intermediate level, so that higher-level students may begin by using the later chapters. These students may also benefit from the confidence gained in mastering the simpler early chapters while still enjoying the content of the stories.

Organization and Features

The readings are grouped into three general themes: Part 1 deals with culture shock, Part 2 with problems that students experience in their first attempts at communicating in English, and Part 3 with coming to understand a new people. Each chapter concentrates on one story, which is supported by a prereading synopsis, postreading activities, and illustrations that depict key elements of the reading. Following the story, short answer questions stimulate thought about the main ideas, cloze exercises and derived forms tables reinforce vocabulary in context, and questions of inference and questions for discussion and writing call for deeper analysis. One chapter includes the more open-ended activity of predicting and writing the end of the story. Since answers are provided in the Appendix, comprehension and vocabulary exercises are as appropriate for self-study as they are for pair or small group work in class.

The layout of the chapters is designed to accommodate readers' interactive text processing: illustrations representing the essence of a story provide a conceptual orientation (top-down processing); the text then provides confirmation and detail (bottom-up processing). Illustrations and icons attract attention and encourage students to guess context and meaning. The use of these pictorial cues allows students to concentrate on language without struggling at the same time to comprehend the situations described in the readings.

Footnotes and chapter glossaries (presented as matching exercises) help students with difficult vocabulary, idioms, and constructions necessary to the story.

Using the Text

Using the text as a primary reader. The *stories* are the heart of *For Here or To Go?* They are designed both to present ideas and perspectives familiar to students and to arouse reaction and reflection.

By focusing on the *story*, students use the grammar they learn in other classes to communicate original ideas and opinions. Because some students are intimidated by a formal approach to grammar, in-class discussions will proceed more freely when grammar awareness becomes incidental and infrequent.

Using the text as a supplementary reader. The stories can be used as a springboard for class-specific activities. Some teachers may elect to use only the stories, replacing the activities with exercises and projects that dovetail with structures and material that their students are studying in other classes.

Using the exercises and activities. The various short comprehension, vocabulary cloze, and matching exercises in each chapter provide practice with and reinforcement of the structures and vocabulary presented in the story. Teachers can expand this vocabulary with semantic clusters or scales showing intensity of synonyms, quantifiers, or qualifiers. Much of the new vocabulary of each chapter is repeated in subsequent stories, thereby providing greater retention through reinforcement. Students should be aware that the vocabulary items may also have other meaning in contexts different from the story. Also, the importance of derived forms can't be overstated in expanding the students' vocabulary beyond the use of one word form. When students learn *boring* as an adjective, they should be shown how it functions as a verb, a noun, and an adjective of the experiencer (*bored*), if possible.

Discussion and writing activities provide the instructor with opportunities for expansion of the language under study. Except for the lowest-level classes, or for those students needing extensive reinforcement before moving on to another context, the array of exercises and activities in each chapter provides a *range* of activities *from which to choose*. Instructors and students *may* find a decreasing need for the chapter activities as they progress through the book. An icon of "the Thinker" appears next to more challenging exercises or activities.

Vocabulary appearing in the text in **bold** carries footnotes on the pages where those words occur. With a few exceptions, these items are not included in the activities. This annotated vocabulary is either not as common or not as important as the basic vocabulary ("Key Words of the Story") in the text, which is reinforced and expanded in the activities. The annotations provide enough information for the student to get through the story.

Students should work together in pairs or groups where their native languages are mixed to ensure that English is the language of communication.

Expansion Ideas

Reading aloud. When starting each new chapter, ask a student to read the story aloud for his or her classmates. The rest of the class should keep their books closed.

Listening. Read the story aloud for students at the start of each new chapter. Again, the rest of the class should keep their books closed. This will give them a feel for the sound and tone of the story. Alternatively, after finishing the chapter, read the story while students read along to reinforce pronunciation, stress, and intonation.

Skits or video making. A more ambitious but highly rewarding project for later in the semester, or when students are quite comfortable with one another, is to have small groups act out a skit representing a story of their choice or one under study at that time. An off-stage (or off-camera) participant can provide voice-over narration to express what the protagonist of a story is thinking, the so-called internal dialogue. Students may want to embellish the story in ways that they find amusing.

Anecdote writing. After reading these stories, many students are motivated to write their own coming-to-America stories. Some students mirror stories in the book; others express very different experiences or perspectives.

References

Carrell, P. L., J. Devine, and D. E. Eskey, eds. 1988. *Interactive Approaches to Second Language Reading*. Cambridge: Cambridge University Press.

Grabe, W., and R. B. Kaplan. 1989. "Writing in a Second Language: Contrastive Rhetoric." In *Richness in Writing*, ed. D. M. Johnson and D. H. Roen. New York: Longman.

Larsen-Freeman, D., and M. H. Long. 1991. *An Introduction to Second Language Acquisition Research*. London: Longman.

Acknowledgments

Several people took great interest in this book, and it is they that I have to thank for encouraging me to prepare it for publication. My wife, Linda D'Amore, urged me on and provided instructional design advice and practical feedback on the stories. (She was, of course, overly critical.) Two colleagues in particular used chapters extensively with their own students who provided valuable feedback: Mary Ann Brady at the Center for English Language and Orientation Programs (CELOP) at Boston University and Newbury College; Terry O'Neil at Roxbury Community College and Bunker Hill Community College. My own students at Boston University, Showa Boston, Simmons College, and Emmanuel College were repeatedly subjected to various experiments with the manuscript. Justine Gamache generously accepted the task of illustrating on absurdly short notice. She brilliantly depicted the stories with elegant yet efficient drawings.

Steven J. Molinsky at Boston University taught me how to think critically about what *should* happen in the second-language classroom versus what has been done in the past. He was also helpful in forming my ideas about this book at its inception and responding constructively to its first draft. I would also like to thank the anonymous reviewers at the University of Michigan Press for their cogent suggestions and the teachers in the Department of English and CELOP at Boston University for their responses to my questions about cultural and linguistic issues in their ESL classes.

Contents

Chapter 1
The American Classroom

Before You Read the Story

Every classroom has rules. These rules are different from **culture** to culture. Miho, who is from Tokyo, Japan, is studying in the United States. She wants to teach English in Japan. Look carefully at the drawings with the story on the following pages. Can you **"read"** the story in these drawings?

culture: the beliefs and behaviors of a social group; their way of life

"read": understand the story in pictures

clarify: to make clear or understandable

The American Classroom

In Japan, I studied English for many years. I knew English well when I began college in the United States, but I was not prepared for American style education. It is very different from Japanese education.

In Japan, students usually listen to the instructor. They ask questions only to **clarify** something they do not understand. They usually do not question or doubt the instructor. They repeat what the instructor tells them. He or she is usually right.

In America, students talk as much as the instructor does, sometimes more. They say what they believe in class (their opinions). Sometimes they disagree with the instructor. Most instructors encourage students to be independent and to think for themselves. In some classes, students critique each other's work. I found the American classroom shocking at first.

The first time an instructor **called on** me to speak in class, I couldn't say anything, so she called on someone else. The second time she called on me, I repeated what she had said. I wanted to **gain her approval**. She told me to say what I believed, not repeat what she had said. Was she **tricking** me or testing me? I didn't know, so I repeated what she had said. She got angry with me and again called on another student. She asked him the same question that she had asked me.

This student spoke for several minutes. In his answer, he disagreed with many things the instructor had said. He was also eating a muffin and drinking coffee—right in class! This behavior was shocking. I thought the student was very rude and disrespectful. But, in fact, the instructor was pleased by his answer. I think the instructor thought that he was the best student because he **spoke up** during every class and gave his opinions.

Now, after several years at an American university, I like the American classroom. I think that I'm even becoming an American

call on: to ask a question of someone in a group

gain approval: to please

trick: to fool or play a game

speak up: to speak voluntarily in a group

student. I speak up in class when I want to, or I just sit and listen when I don't have anything to say. My English has **definitely** improved a lot because I have to talk in class. I bring tea or soda into afternoon classes to keep me awake—when I'd rather be taking a nap. I can leave the classroom during a class to use the rest room. In Japan, I might have to wait to go, perhaps for several hours. Also, American students sometimes come to class late. I could never come to class late in Japan.

    In general, I think students in American classrooms are more comfortable than students in Japanese classrooms because they have more freedom. They can *do* and *say* whatever they want. However, I don't want to be a teacher in America. More freedom for students means less control—and more **headaches**—for teachers.

definitely:
certainly; without a doubt

headache: a pain in the head; trouble

What's in the Story?

Which *ideas* are in or related to Miho's story? Circle them. Then compare your answers with a classmate.

Japan   New York   behavior   noise   American education
opinions   classroom pollution   argument   computers

What's the Story About?

Write short answers to these questions. Try to write *more* than one or two words.

1. Who tells this story?_____

    _____

2. In Miho's first American class, what made her uncomfortable?

    _____

3. How are Japanese students different from American students?

   _____

4. How are Japanese teachers different from American teachers?

   _____

5. Which type of classroom does Miho like more now? _____

   _____

6. What subject is Miho studying? _____

   _____

7. What does Miho want to do when she finishes college? _____

   _____

8. Do you think Miho will be good at this profession? Why? _____

   _____

Using the Best Word

clue: a small piece of information that helps you understand or solve something

Circle the best word to complete each sentence. The vocabulary comes from the story you have just read. Other words in the sentence(s) give you **clues** to (help you guess) the meanings of the missing word(s).

Verbs	*Nouns*	*Adjectives*
critique	control	comfortable
disagree	freedom	disrespectful
doubt	nap	independent
encourage	opinion	pleased
question		prepared
repeat		rude
		shocking

1. In Japan, Miho accepted everything the teachers said. She never *questioned / repeated / encouraged* the teacher. It would be

prepared / independent / disrespectful to *control / disagree / nap* with the teacher.

2. American teachers want their students to speak up in class. They *critique / encourage / control* their students to participate in class discussions. They often want to know what the students think, their *naps / freedom / opinions*. They do not want students to simply *repeat / rude / critique* what they said. Therefore, students should come to class *prepared / shocking / comfortable*.

3. Generally, American schools do not teach students to believe what everyone else believes. Rather, they encourage students to be *shocking / freedom / independent* thinkers. Students have the *doubt / freedom / opinion* to believe what they want.

4. Students, especially in college, can learn from their peers and from the teacher. Sometimes they *critique / repeat / doubt* each other's work.

5. Miho can do what she wants in class. She can speak up, be quiet, or sometimes even eat or drink. At first, this behavior was *pleased / comfortable / shocking* to her. But now, she is more *rude / disrespectful / comfortable* in class.

6. Although she often gets tired in class, she can't take a *control / opinion / nap*. Sleeping might be *rude / prepared / disagree*, even in an American class.

7. Miho's teachers are now very *disrespectful / prepared / pleased* when she speaks up in class.

8. Miho thinks that American students have a lot of freedom in class but that their teachers have less *freedom / opinion / control* than in Japanese classrooms.

What Do You Think?

With a classmate or in small groups, discuss the following questions.

1. What are classrooms like in your country? For example, how do students behave and what do teachers expect of students?

2. Which classrooms are better for learning, the ones in America or the ones where you come from? Explain.

3. American classrooms were "shocking" to Miho. What was shocking to you when you first arrived in the United States?

4. Imagine that an American college student is going to your country. Describe his or her first day in class. What would you tell this student to prepare him or her for the first day?

5. In Japan, teachers often dress **formally.** Men wear a suit and tie. How do teachers dress in your country?

6. In Japan, the teacher's desk or **podium** at the front of the class is often raised up higher than the floor of the class. Where do teachers sit or stand in classrooms in your country?

7. A popular **proverb** says, "When in Rome, do as the Romans do." What do you think this means? Is there an example of behavior that fits this proverb in the story?

After discussing all of the questions, pick one of them to write about individually. Write your answer in one paragraph.

formally: for business or other serious activities

podium: a tall, narrow desk that a speaker stands behind when speaking in front of a large group of people

proverb: old, common saying that gives advice, a warning, or an observation

Key Words of the Story

Match the vocabulary words on the left with their meanings on the right. Write the word number on the line next to its meaning. (Dots (•) separate syllables. Stress marks (ʹ) indicate the syllable stressed in pronunciation of the word.)

key: important

V = verb; **N** = noun;
Adj = adjective

1. pre•páred (**Adj**)

2. doubt (**V**)

3. re•péat (**V**)

4. o•pín•ion (**N**)

5. dis•a•grée (**V**)

6. en•cóur•age (**V**)

7. in•de•pén•dent (Adj)

8. cri•tíque (**V**)

9. shóck•ing (Adj)

10. rude (Adj)

11. dis•re•spéct•ful (Adj)

12. pleased (Adj)

13. nap (N)

14. cóm•fort•able (Adj)

15. frée•dom (N)

16. con•tról (N)

a. ___ to say or do again

b. ___ to not agree

c. ___ completely unexpected; surprising

d. ___ happy; satisfied

e. ___ not showing respect

f. ___ not showing proper manners

g. ___ one's personal thought or perspective

h. ___ at ease; free of stress or tension

i. ___ a short sleep during the day

j. ___ acting as an individual; not controlled by others

k. ___ to give help, hope, or courage

l. ___ ability to make choices, decisions

m. ___ to read for accuracy or faults; to review

n. ___ power to command or restrain

o. ___ to not believe or trust

p. ___ ready

Derived Forms

There are eight *parts of speech* in English. These are categories of words. Each category of word, or part of speech, does something different. Four of these parts of speech are given in the table: *verb, noun, adjective,* and *adverb*. Many words have more than one form. That is, they may have forms for more than one part of speech. These different forms of the same word are called *derived forms*. For example, here are the forms of the word confuse:

The teacher *confused* Maria.	*Use:* verb form
The instructions caused *confusion*.	*Use:* noun form
The teacher was *confusing*. Maria was *confused*.	*Use:* adjective forms
The teacher *confusingly* explained the grammar.	*Use:* adverb form

A little grammar: *Verbs* do things. They describe action or being. *Nouns* are people, places, things, or ideas. There are *count* nouns (pens, keys, students) and *noncount* nouns (milk, air, confusion, freedom). *Adjectives* describe things (nouns or pronouns). *Adverbs* describe actions (verbs). They also modify adjectives or other adverbs.

The table shows some vocabulary from chapter 1. Fill in the different forms of each word in the blank boxes. If a box contains a line, there is no word form for you to fill in. Some of them have been done for you already. You can use an English-English (not a bilingual) dictionary.

Verb	Noun	Adjective	Adverb
——————	independence	independent	
	freedom		freely
control		controlled/controlling	——————
		pleased/pleasing	pleasingly
comfort			comfortably

Chapter 2
The Escalator

Before You Read the Story

Sometimes **unfamiliar** things frighten us. Later, when we learn more about them, we feel foolish because they're **commonplace** and **harmless**. Lieu, who is from Vietnam, remembers when she first saw an escalator. Look carefully at the drawings with the story on the following pages. Can you "read" the story in these drawings?

escalator: moving (mechanical) steel stairs

unfamiliar: not familiar; not known

commonplace: ordinary; not unusual

harmless: not dangerous

the rest of: all the others

in all: total

corridor: a long hallway

• • • • • • • • • • • • • • • •

The Escalator

My first experience in the United States was very embarrassing. I still feel foolish talking about it. The story makes me think of how different my country is from the United States.

I'm 19 years old now. When I left my country, Vietnam, I was just 10. My mother and I were flying to Boston to be with **the rest of** our family. The flight was very long, over 30 hours **in all**. We went through Customs and Immigration at the airport, then a lady who worked for the airport, Gail, led us to the waiting area. My father, brother, and uncles were waiting there. We had to walk down several **corridors**.

At the end of the corridor, I saw the moving steel stairs, the escalator, and I got scared. Actually, I screamed. "Do I have to go down it?" I asked Gail. But she didn't understand me. I asked her again and again, but she still didn't understand. Of course, I was speaking Vietnamese. I didn't know that Gail didn't speak Vietnamese. I pointed to the escalator and started crying. She understood me then. I screamed again and **backed away**.

I had never seen an escalator before. It was very frightening **at first**. This one made **hissing** and scratching noises. It was moving as fast as a train, and it seemed as big and heavy as one too. I didn't want this metal monster to **suck** me in and eat me.

Unlike the escalator, Gail was gentle and kind. She had a soft, sweet voice. Unfortunately, the hissing and scratching of the escalator drowned out her soft, sweet voice. She put her arm around me and talked to me. I didn't understand her, but she sounded nicer than the escalator. My mother didn't understand the lady either, but she didn't seem afraid of the escalator. My mother was very brave.

As Gail talked, she tried to pull me toward the escalator. She kept talking to me as she walked onto the top stair. Then she started to go down. It was killing her! The escalator was sucking her in! Someone help this nice lady! Help!

I couldn't believe it. Gail was running back up the stairs. She escaped! But what happened? She was just showing me how safe the escalator was. Walk onto the step and it does all the work.

back away: to move backward; to retreat

at first: in the beginning

hiss: the noise a tire makes when it is losing air

suck: to pull toward (as liquid through a straw)

spread: to move far apart

handrail: the long piece you hold onto along a stair

get off: to exit something moving such as a train, bus, or bicycle

It's easy. She tried again to pull me toward the top stair. When I got close to the stair, I closed my eyes and put only one foot on the top stair. My legs **spread** apart and I fell over backward. I screamed again and crawled off the top stair. After this, Gail got impatient, said something to my mother, then walked away down the corridor.

I was never going to get down the escalator alive now. I was never going to see the rest of my family. The escalator was going to cut off my feet. That was the price for seeing my family, my feet.

Finally, my mother grabbed my hand and walked right onto the escalator with me. I didn't have time to fight, but I did have time to scream again, a long scream. I screamed until I saw some other kids pointing at me and laughing. They were going down the same escalator with their parents. The parents laughed too. I watched them laugh, then, suddenly, I realized that I was going down. I didn't even have to scream. I was okay. And I still had my feet!

There I was, on the escalator, grabbing the **handrail** with both hands. I was a little relieved. Then I looked down to the bottom of the long escalator. I was going down fast. How do I **get off**? No one showed me how to get off. I panicked and saw the bottom getting closer and closer. I saw my family waiting for me. They were laughing too, especially my younger brother. My father saw that I was scared. Near the bottom, I closed my eyes and screamed again. He came up to the edge of the escalator, grabbed me, and picked me up. It felt good to get off of that thing. He carried me away from the noise of the escalator, then put me down. My whole family was together again for the first time in a long time.

Today, I can walk onto an escalator while reading a magazine or drinking a soda, without even looking. I still can't believe I was so afraid of it at one time. The escalator in the airport that first day prepared me for future experiences in the U.S. I had other frightening experiences living in this country. Fortunately, none was as bad as the escalator.

What's in the Story?

Which *ideas* are in or related to Lieu's story? Circle them. Then compare your answers with a classmate.

teacher   feeling afraid work student   screams   Vietnam
escalator   classroom   sleep phone   feeling foolish family

What's the Story About?

Write short answers to these questions. Try to write *more* than one or two words.

1. Where does Lieu come from? _____

   _____

2. Where does she live now? _____

   _____

3. How long has she lived here? _____

   _____

4. Why did she move? _____

   _____

5. What frightened Lieu? Why? _____

   _____

6. Who is Gail? _____

   _____

7. What did Lieu do when she saw the frightening thing for the first

   time? _____

   _____

8. Who was with her when she was frightened? _____

_____

9. Did she overcome her fear (is she still afraid of escalators)? _____

_____

10. In the end, what did the escalator represent? _____

_____

Guessing Meaning

Guess the correct words from the following list to fill in the blanks. Use the right *form* of each word (verb or adjective) and use the right tense of verbs (past, present). The vocabulary comes from the story you have just read. Other words in the sentence(s) give you clues to (help you guess) the meaning(s) of the missing word(s).

Verbs	*Adjectives*
crawl	brave
drown out	embarrassing
escape	foolish
grab	gentle
have to	impatient
panic	relieved
prepare	scared, afraid
realize	
scream	

1. Lieu had no choice; the escalator was the only way to get down to where her family was. She _____ _____ take it.

2. When Lieu fell down in front of other people, her face turned red. It was _____ for her. Later, she felt _____ for being _____ of the escalator. There was really no danger.

3. Lieu thought that Gail had died in the escalator. A moment later, she _____ that Gail was alive when she walked back up the stairs. Gail was _____ to walk on the escalator like that.

4. When Lieu fell on the escalator, she _____ loudly then _____ off the top stair on her hands and knees.

5. When a fire suddenly starts in a building, people often scream and _____. They want to _____ the danger fast.

6. Lieu was _____ when she got off the escalator.

7. Lieu was not afraid of Gail because the kind lady was very _____ with her. However, the noise from the escalator _____ _____ Gail's soft and sweet voice.

8. Gail didn't want to wait for Lieu to go down the escalator. She became _____ with Lieu.

9. Lieu's mother _____ Lieu's hand and pulled her onto the escalator.

10. The escalator experience _____ Lieu for many other new experiences in the United States.

What Do You Think?

With a classmate or in small groups, discuss the following questions.

1. What was the first strange sight (such as an escalator) that you saw in the United States? Did it frighten you? Was your experience similar to Lieu's?
2. How did you come to the United States, by car, bus, boat, or plane? What was your arrival like? Was it happy, sad, frightening, or exciting? Describe how you felt.
3. Describe a strange experience you have had. For students from Japan, for example, a strange experience could be seeing people drive on the right side of the road in the United States or seeing people hug, kiss, and hold hands in public. For students from a desert climate, snow could be a strange sight.

After discussing all of the questions, pick one of them to write about individually. Write your answer in one paragraph.

Key Words of the Story

Match the vocabulary words on the left with their meanings on the right. Write the word number on the line next to its meaning. (Dots (•) separate syllables. Stress marks (´) indicate the syllable stressed in pronunciation of the word.)

1. fríght•en (V)

2. em•bár•rass•ing (Adj)

3. fóol•ish (Adj)

4. have to (V)

5. scared, afraid (Adj)

6. scream (V)

7. gén•tle (Adj)

8. drown out (V)

9. brave (Adj)

10. es•cápe (V)

11. pán•ic (V)

12. crawl (V)

13. im•pá•tient (Adj)

14. ré•al•ize (V)

15. grab (V)

16. re•líeved (Adj)

17. pre•páre (V)

a. ___ to be louder than

b. ___ to make ready

c. ___ delicate (not harsh or violent)

d. ___ feeling in danger

e. ___ to take suddenly with the hands

f. ___ making one feel bad, self conscious in front of others

g. ___ to make afraid

h. ___ not patient; do not like waiting; restless

i. ___ to move on hands and knees

j. ___ must

k. ___ to yell or to cry out loudly

l. ___ to become aware; to recognize

m. ___ at ease; without pressure

n. ___ silly; stupid

o. ___ having no fear

p. ___ to get away from danger

q. ___ to feel sudden fear and get excited

Derived Forms

The table shows some vocabulary from chapter 2. Fill in the different forms of each word in the blank boxes. You can use an English-English (not a bilingual) dictionary. See page 9 in chapter 1 for more explanation.

Verb	Noun	Adjective	Adverb
escape		escaped	————
	realization	————	————
	embarrassment		embarrassingly
		prepared	————
	relief	relieved/relieving	————
fool			foolishly

Chapter 3
The Core of the "Big Apple"

Before You Read the Story

A visit to a foreign city is an exciting experience. Sometimes the city is very different from what you expected. Reza is from a small town in Iran. He remembers his first visit to New York City. Look carefully at the drawings with the story on the following pages. Can you "read" the story in these drawings?

core: the center (and the part of an apple that you can't eat)

Big Apple: a popular nickname (or familiar name used in informal situations) for New York City. The title of this chapter is a wordplay referring to the undesirable part of New York.

Midwest: the middle part of the United States (Ohio, Illinois, Kansas, etc.)

exchange: to trade

lucky: fortunate; in a good situation

• • • • • • • • • • • • • • • • •

The Core of the "Big Apple"

When I was a child in Iran, many of my friends dreamed of visiting Disneyland. I dreamed about visiting New York City. I read books about the city and saw it in movies. It seemed like a wonderful place to me. *Breakfast at Tiffany's*, with the beautiful actress Audrey Hepburn, was my favorite movie about life in New York.

My father had gone to college in Ohio, a state in the **Midwest**. He studied electrical engineering and brought back many books, magazines, and memories from the U.S. Before I could read English, I used to look at one of his books about New York. It was large and had many photographs of the city. When he returned home to Iran, he and his friends regularly **exchanged** books, newspapers, and, later, American movies on video. Some of these things are illegal or very difficult to get in Iran.

I had some cousins who lived in New York. I knew I would visit there someday. I thought that they were **lucky** to live there. New

York has great art museums, buildings like the Empire State Building, expensive shops on Fifth Avenue like Tiffany's, famous hotels like the Plaza, great monuments like the Statue of Liberty and Ellis Island, and Central Park. In photographs and movies, the buildings are so tall that the streets below look like deep valleys. There are so many yellow taxicabs that the streets **flow** like yellow rivers. I had heard so much about New York that it didn't seem like a real place. Instead, it seemed like a dream. I couldn't wait to get to the city where everyone was rich, beautiful, and elegant.

My parents sent me to visit New York when I was about twenty years old. When I finally arrived there, I stayed with my cousins. They lived in Jersey City, which is across the Hudson River in the state of New Jersey. It's only a few minutes by subway from **Manhattan.** I was so excited that I couldn't sleep. "There are so many things I want to see here," I told my cousins.

They told me, "Reza, you shouldn't go to these places alone. We'll go into the city together this weekend. New York can be very dangerous. There are purse snatchers, muggers, prostitutes, drug addicts, and crazy people everywhere."

flow: to move smoothly, like water

Manhattan: There are five parts, or "boroughs," to New York City. Manhattan is the most famous part. People usually mean Manhattan when they say New York City.

entire: whole

I couldn't believe what my cousins had told me. The next day, I went out alone because they were working. I know they told me, "Wait until the weekend," but I couldn't wait anymore. I had waited my **entire** life to see New York.

downtown: usually, the busy center of town

I took the subway under the Hudson River and got off in the middle of **downtown** Manhattan. The trains had paint on them called "**graffiti**." Some of the windows were broken out, and many of the lights in the subway station were also broken or dark. There was **vandalism** in the subways and on the streets.

graffiti: writing with paint on walls in public places (a form of vandalism)

vandalism: the destruction of property

The streets were crowded with people. I couldn't walk without bumping into them. Everyone was in a hurry. People didn't talk to each other very much or look at each other. Cars, buses, and taxis honked their horns incessantly and wouldn't slow down for pedestrians. The streets were dirty with trash. The wind lifted pieces of paper into the air, and they flew high above the street. Some kids carried "boom boxes" that played music very loudly. Everything was loud. I couldn't hear myself think.

People dressed very strangely here, and women acted like men. Some people dressed very badly. Their shirts were hanging out of their pants, or they wore shorts that looked like **underwear**. Many women wore clothes that revealed their **bare** arms, legs, lower necks, and more! Women in Iran could never dress like this. A woman in the subway came up to me and asked me to light her cigarette. Women in Iran don't smoke in public and don't usually approach a strange man. In fact, they cannot be seen alone in public with a man unless he is a relative.

I must tell you that Audrey Hepburn in *Breakfast at Tiffany's* did smoke cigarettes. However, the woman in the subway did not look anything like Audrey Hepburn. Hepburn looked quite elegant with a cigarette in the film. In fact, she looked elegant doing anything.

I was shocked and disappointed. This wasn't the New York that I had read about or imagined. I returned home to my cousins' apartment before dinner. I told them about my day. They told me that they didn't like to go into the city at all. They usually stayed home when they weren't working. In fact, they wanted to move to a state out west, maybe California or Arizona.

I had come a long way to get to New York. I had to explore it. I had to give it a chance. I couldn't return home to my father and tell him that New York was not a wonderful or exciting place. So I went out by myself again. I took a small map of the city that my father had given me.

On that second day exploring the city, I discovered beautiful old buildings, green parks, and quiet, friendly neighborhoods. The streets were safe, and there was interesting activity everywhere. I discovered that New York is an international city with all kinds of people. I heard many other languages spoken, including **Farsi** (the official language of Iran). At night, street musicians played jazz on many busy street corners. I love jazz. Several times people answered my questions and helped me when I was lost. Two women from New York University walked with me to a subway station. They helped me get on the right train. On the way, they asked me questions about Middle East politics because they were studying political science in college.

Then, at the subway station, a man opened the door for me. At first I thought he was very kind. Later, I learned that he wanted money from me because he was **homeless**. I had never seen

underwear: the clothes (often white) worn under our shirts, pants, and dresses

bare: without clothes; showing skin

Farsi: the Persian language

homeless: people who have no home and live on the street

anyone beg for money on the street in Iran. It was strange to see this, but the man was not dangerous.

New York was very different from my town in Iran. It was much bigger, and the people acted very differently. These differences can be shocking at first but also exciting. There seemed to be fewer rules in New York. People had more freedoms, especially the women. Many people say that **New Yorkers** are rude. I don't agree. They are cautious because it is so crowded and a little dangerous there. They **mind their own business**, but they're not rude to each other (except the drivers). Not all the areas of the city are dirty and dangerous. In fact, when I learned about the city **firsthand**, I realized that it wasn't exactly the city I had seen in movies or read about in books, but it also wasn't the dangerous place that frightened my cousins.

I teach math in Iran now, but I will never forget my first trip to New York. That experience prepared me for travel to other cities of the world. I am now more realistic in my expectations. I know that places are not actually as they appear in **novels**, magazines, movies, or even travel books.

New Yorkers: residents of New York

mind one's own business: to keep to oneself and not take interest in what others are doing (to be polite)

firsthand: from one's own personal experience

novel: a book of fiction (not a true story)

What's in the Story?

Which *ideas* are in or related to Reza's story? Circle them. Then compare your answers with a classmate.

exploring a place   Grand Canyon   New York   lake
movies and television   dangerous places   opinions   food
disappointment   subway

What's the Story About?

Write short answers to these questions. Try to write *more* than one or two words.

1. Why is Reza in New York? _____

   _____

2. With whom is he staying? Where? _____

   _____

3. What did Reza imagine about New York? _____

   _____

4. Do his cousins like this city? How do they feel? _____

   _____

5. What does he like about New York? _____

   _____

6. What does he not like about New York? _____

   _____

7. What does Reza think about this city *after* exploring it? _____

   _____

8. In the end, how has New York City changed Reza? _____

   _____

Guessing Meaning

Guess the correct words from the following list to fill in the blanks.
Use the right *form* of each word (verb, noun, adjective, or adverb) and
use the right tense of verbs (past, present). The vocabulary comes
from the story you have just read. Other words in the sentence(s) give
you clues to (help you guess) the meaning(s) of the missing word(s).

Verbs	*Nouns*	*Adjectives*	*Adverbs*
approach	chance	cautious	exactly
beg	expectation	crowded	incessantly
discover	pedestrian	dangerous	
dream		disappointed	
explore		elegant	
reveal		exciting	
		favorite	
		real	
		realistic	
		wonderful	

1. New York was all Reza thought about in Iran. He _____ that
   he would one day visit the city. When he was 20, he got the
   _____ to go.

2. At first, New York seemed dirty, noisy, and dangerous to Reza. It
   was not what he had imagined. He was sad and
   _____.

3. Reza had read and learned a lot about New York while he was still
   in Iran. He had an _____ of New York that it was a
   _____ place.

4. In books and movies, New York did not seem like a _____
   place. In fact, Reza discovered that the movies were not

_____ in their description of the city. They did not

show the city _____ as it is.

5. Audrey Hepburn was Reza's _____ American

   actress. She looked beautiful and _____, no matter

   what she did.

6. Reza walked around New York for several days. He

   _____ many neighborhoods and _____

   many fascinating sights.

7. New York is not boring at all. It's quite _____.

8. After experiencing New York firsthand, Reza didn't think it was as

   _____ as his cousins had said. However, he was

   _____ about where he went. He didn't want trouble.

9. Reza found New Yorkers to be private. They didn't regularly

   _____ strangers on the street or talk to each other a lot,

   except for the homeless, who sometimes _____ for

   money.

10. Cars seemed to honk their horns without stop. They honked

    _____(**Adv**) at _____ (N) trying

    to cross the streets. And the sidewalks were so _____

    that it was difficult for pedestrians to walk without bumping into

    each other.

11. American clothes _____ more bare skin on women than

    clothes worn by women in Iran.

Adv = adverb

What Do You Think?

With a classmate or in small groups, discuss the following questions.

1. What cities outside of your native country have you visited? Are you living in a "foreign" city now?
2. Before you visited a foreign city, what did you think it was going to be like? When you visited it, was it like you had expected? How?
3. Do you like to explore new places the way Reza does in the story? How are you the same or different?
4. Imagine someone is going to visit your hometown. What would you tell him or her about it? How would you prepare this person for the dangerous and wonderful parts of the city?

After discussing all of the questions, pick one of them to write about individually. Write your answer in one paragraph.

Key Words of the Story

Match the vocabulary words on the left with their meanings on the right. Write the word number on the line next to its meaning. (Dots (•) separate syllables. Stress marks (ʹ) indicate the syllable stressed in pronunciation of the word.)

1. ex•péct (V)

2. dream (V)

3. re•véal (V)

4. ap•próach (V)

5. ex•plóre (V)

6. dis•cóv•er (V)

7. beg (V)

8. ex•cít•ing (Adj)

9. wón•der•ful (Adj)

10. fá•vor•ite (Adj)

11. real (Adj)

12. él•e•gant (Adj)

13. dán•ger•ous (Adj)

14. crówd•ed (Adj)

15. dis•ap•póinted (Adj)

16. cáu•tious (Adj)

17. re•al•ís•tic (Adj)

18. in•cés•sant•ly (Adv)

19. ex•áct•ly (Adv)

20. ex•pec•tá•tion (N)

21. pe•dés•tri•an (N)

a. ____ to ask in great need (as for money)

b. ____ to travel through an area in order to discover things

c. ____ to move toward someone or something

d. ____ to show (not hide)

e. ____ to find something; learn something

f. ____ to form a mental picture of something

g. ____ to look forward to something; to think something is likely to happen

h. ____ reasonable; probable

i. ____ not getting what was expected or wanted

j. ____ graceful; tasteful; stylish

k. ____ too many people in one place

l. ____ careful

m. ____ unusually great

n. ____ actual; existing in reality

o. ____ having much activity; stimulating

22. chance (N)

p. ___ preferred; first choice

q. ___ not safe

r. ___ precisely; without difference

s. ___ without stopping

t. ___ opportunity

u. ___ a thought about something likely in the future

v. ___ someone walking on the street

Derived Forms

The table shows some vocabulary from chapter 3. Fill in the different forms of each word in the blank boxes. You can use an English-English (not a bilingual) dictionary. See page 9 in chapter 1 for more explanation.

Verb	Noun	Adjective	Adverb
	revelation		revealingly
excite		excited/exciting	
	exploration		———
disappoint		disappointed	
	discovery		———
———			dangerously

Chapter 4
Back to School

Before You Read the Story

Daniil is from Moscow, Russia. He was a doctor there. When he came to the United States, he could not work as a doctor. He had to go back to school in the United States for many years before working as a doctor here. Studying as an adult student in Boston was very different from studying as a young student in Russia. Look carefully at the drawings with the story on the following pages. Can you "read" the story in these drawings?

• • • • • • • • • • • • • • • •

Back to School

I came to the U.S. about twelve years ago. I spoke no English, not a word. I didn't want to come here either, but many members of my family already lived here. My wife and I arrived with **nothing more than** some clothes and personal things.

We **moved in** with some friends and family. We shared the bottom floor of a large house in Brookline, Massachusetts. Brookline **borders** Boston and is a very nice town. Many doctors, lawyers, and professors live here—many rich people too. We weren't rich, and we didn't have good jobs here. In fact, at first I worked as a **janitor** in a local hospital. It was boring work, and I didn't like it.

nothing more than: only

move in: to go to live with

border: to be next to; to share a boundary or border

janitor: the person who cleans the floors, etc.

31

one by one: first one of us left, then another, then another, etc.

license: legal and professional permission

practice medicine: to work as a doctor seeing patients

center for adult education: a school that offers low-cost classes similar to college but does not award college degrees (such as B.A., B.S., M.B.A., etc.)

You see, in Russia (which was called the Soviet Union before 1991) I was a doctor, a respected ophthalmologist. An ophthalmologist is a doctor who takes care of people's eyes. I also did certain eye operations in Russia that Americans were not yet doing. But I had many problems in Russia because I am Jewish. Some of my Jewish friends and family were in trouble with the Russian authorities (the government and the police). They weren't criminals, but their political and religious activities and writing worried the authorities. So **one by one**, we left.

I couldn't work as a doctor in the U.S. because I didn't have a **license** to **practice medicine** here. I didn't even speak English. So my friends registered me in ESL classes at a local **center for adult education**.

I started taking English classes a few weeks later. My classmates were from many other countries, such as El Salvador, Colombia, the Philippines, Vietnam, Thailand, and, of course, Russia. Some were young, and others were old, like me.

The teacher, Terry, was much younger than most of the students. This surprised me. He was a kid! What can I learn from a kid? At first, he didn't teach us very much English. He smiled a lot and said, "Have fun." Fun in class? He also told us to talk to

each other in pairs or small groups. But what did *we* know? We couldn't understand each other very well at all.

"it's up to you":
it's your choice; you choose

Maybe *he* didn't know English grammar. I argued with him about the answers to some grammar exercises. He said, "Sometimes there's *more* than one answer. **It's up to you.**" In Russia, when I was in school, the teacher told the students the right answer. We accepted his or her answer then. We did not spend time talking to each other in class or discussing *more* than one possible answer.

teenage: between the ages of 13 and 19

After some time, however, I started to like my English classes. Talking to my classmates was better than doing grammar lessons. I liked talking to my classmates. Some of them had very interesting and sometimes tragic experiences. One man, from Cali, Colombia, had lost his wife and **teenage** son. They were killed by criminals. He loved his town, Cali, and did not want to leave it. But he had no choice. He had no family and only a few friends in Boston. His story made me very sad. There were other students that I didn't understand at all, and so I didn't work with them in class. But that was okay. There were a lot of us.

Terry sat down and talked to each of the small groups in class as we did our grammar exercises. I realized that he was smart and that he did know English grammar well. But his way of teaching was very different from a Russian teacher's way. Every day he said, "Don't memorize rules. Learn to think for yourselves about English. Learn to *use* English by speaking it a lot in class."

When I was in Russia, America seemed like a dream. But when I first came here, it seemed like a nightmare. Life here was very different and confusing (there was too much of everything, too much waste). I have learned many things since then. Classes are more exciting because teachers want students to be comfortable and have fun. They also teach students *how* to think, not just *what* to think. I still miss some things about Russian life though.

I spent several years learning English in order to get a license to practice medicine in the U.S. I had to take many medical exams. Finally, I'm working as a doctor again, an ophthalmologist in Brookline. My story is a little funny though. You see, most of my patients now are Russians who know almost no English, so we speak Russian!

What's in the Story?

Which *ideas* are in or related to Daniil's story? Circle them. Then compare your answers with a classmate.

coffee	medicine	flight	adult student	sickness
Japan	marriage	cars	ESL classes	babies
Russia	discussions	Jewish		

What's the Story About?

Write short answers to these questions. Try to write *more* than one or two words.

1. Who is Daniil? _____

   _____

2. Why did he come to America? _____

   _____

3. What is his profession (his work)? _____

_____

4. Where did he learn English? When? _____

_____

5. Who is Terry? _____

_____

6. What did Daniil think of Terry? Did he like him? _____

_____

7. What did Terry do in class with his students? _____

_____

8. What did Daniil learn about American education? _____

_____

True or False

Are the following statements about the story true or false? Circle T (true) or F (false).

T   F   1. Daniil studied English in Russia.
T   F   2. Daniil used to be a policeman.
T   F   3. Daniil is married.
T   F   4. Terry is a doctor who works with Daniil.
T   F   5. Daniil always liked his English classes.
T   F   6. Terry is a teenage janitor in Cali, Colombia.
T   F   7. Later, Daniil enjoyed the group discussions with his classmates.
T   F   8. Life in Russia was confusing, and there was a lot of waste.

Guessing Meaning

Guess the correct word from the following list to fill in the blanks. Use the right *form* of each word (verb, noun, or adjective) and use the right tense of verbs (past, present). The vocabulary comes from the story you have just read. Other words in the sentence(s) give you clues to (help you guess) the meaning(s) of the missing word(s).

Verbs	*Nouns*	*Adjectives*
argue	activity	boring
memorize	kid	confusing
register	nightmare	smart
share	pair	tragic
surprise	waste	
worry		

1. Daniil _____ for ESL classes at a school.

2. Daniil doesn't live alone. He _____ a house with several other family members.

3. One of Daniil's classmates had a very sad, _____ story. His wife and son were killed.

4. The teacher was very young. This _____ Daniil because he expected someone older. He thought Terry was a _____.

5. At first, Daniil _____ with Terry about English grammar. Later, he realized that Terry was _____ and that his classes were exciting, not _____.

6. Some political _____ and writing _____ the authorities.

7. Terry didn't want students to _____ grammar rules.

   He wanted them to talk, especially in _____ or small

   groups.

8. When Daniil first arrived in America, he thought life here was

   complicated and _____. There was more than he

   needed here, too much _____. Instead of a dream, it

   seemed more like a _____.

What Do You Think?

With a classmate or in small groups, discuss the following questions.

1. Do you remember a teacher that you *didn't* like? Why didn't you
   like him or her? Did you do well in the class?
2. Should a teacher be older than the students? Explain.
3. Do you like studying English grammar? Do you think it helps
   you?
4. Do you like working in pairs or small groups of students in your
   English class? Is it better for you than listening to the teacher
   give a lesson?
5. Do American teachers give students more choices in the classroom? If so, is this a good idea?
6. Do you think Americans waste a lot of things (e.g., food, paper,
   packaging)? Do people waste these things in your country?

After discussing all of the questions, pick one of them to write about
individually. Write your answer in one paragraph.

Key Words of the Story

Match the vocabulary words on the left with their meanings on the right. Write the word number on the line next to its meaning. (Dots (•) separate syllables. Stress marks (ʹ) indicate the syllable stressed in pronunciation of the word.)

1. share (V)

2. bór•ing (Adj)

3. ac•tív•i•ty (N)

4. wór•ry (V)

5. rég•is•ter (V)

6. sur•príse (V)

7. kid (N)

8. pair (N)

9. ár•gue (V)

10. trág•ic (Adj)

11. smart (Adj)

12. mém•o•rize (V)

13. níght•mare (N)

14. con•fús•ing (Adj)

15. waste (N)

a. ___ intelligent

b. ___ to disagree forcefully (in speech)

c. ___ excess or extra amount that is not used

d. ___ difficult to understand

e. ___ a very bad dream or experience

f. ___ to amaze or make aware unexpectedly

g. ___ very sad; unfortunate

h. ___ to officially sign up for something

i. ___ two of something that work together

j. ___ to remember in detail

k. ___ informal word for a young person

l. ___ to feel concern or anxiety

m. ___ actions and involvement

n. ___ to divide and use in common with others

o. ___ uninteresting; not exciting

Derived Forms

The table shows some vocabulary from chapter 4. Fill in the different forms of each word in the blank boxes. You can use an English-English (not a bilingual) dictionary. See page 9 in chapter 1 for more explanation.

Verb	Noun	Adjective	Adverb
	worry		
	boredom	boring/bored	
act		active	
surprise			surprisingly
	confusion	confusing/confused	
waste		wasted	———

Chapter 5
"Anything Else with That?"

Before You Read the Story

As you know, it's not easy to use a second language in the "**real world**." Evangelina, who is from the Dominican Republic, writes about how the easiest activities become difficult or impossible in a country where you cannot speak the native language. Look carefully at the drawings with the story on the following pages. Can you "read" the story in these drawings?"

"real world": actual daily life experience

get by: to accomplish with minimal effort

by myself: alone

run errands: to take care of small personal business, such as mailing letters, shopping, etc.

• • • • • • • • • • • • • • •
"Anything Else with That?"

When I first came to the United States, I stayed with my sister and her husband. They lived in Charlestown, a part of Boston. I didn't speak any English then, so they had to do everything for me. At first, I was even too afraid to go to the store.

My sister taught me some common words and expressions in English. We practiced English at home: she acted as a store clerk or restaurant waitress, and I acted as the customer and ordered what I wanted. I practiced ordering coffee in English: "One medium coffee with cream, no sugar, please." I practiced asking for someone on the telephone: "Hello, may I please speak to Rita?" English was easy. I could say everything that I needed to say. But I had never practiced with anyone else.

After about a month, I thought I had learned enough English to **get by**. I decided to go out of the apartment **by myself** and **run**

some errands. I wanted to go to Bunker Hill Community College, near our apartment, to get information about ESL courses.

First, I stopped to get some coffee. I walked into Joe's **Donuts.** There was a line of people waiting to buy donuts and coffee. It was a very popular place. I waited in line for several minutes. **In my head,** I practiced my order: "One medium coffee with cream, no sugar, please." This was my first test of using English in the "real world." No problem, right?

When it was my turn, I said to the man behind the **counter,** "One medium coffee with cream, no sugar, please." He smiled and said, "Sure." My sister had told me that Americans say "sure" a lot. It means "okay." When the man gave me the coffee, he smiled again and said something to me. "Excuse me?" I said. He said it again. I **had no idea** what he said. It was just noise coming from his mouth. Maybe he asked me a question. I didn't know. I think

donut: short for doughnut, which is a sweet pastry

in my head: in my mind; to myself

counter: the table in any store or restaurant where customers pay or order something

have no idea: did not know at all

change: the
amount the clerk
gives back to the
customer; here,
about four dollars
($5 minus price of
coffee)

handle: the part of
the door used to
open or close it

"hon": short for
honey; an
affectionate, very
informal and
familiar name for a
friend (usually
female)

he was waiting for me to answer. I'm sure he was waiting for
something in addition to the money for the coffee. I got nervous
and put a five dollar bill on the counter to pay for my coffee (which
was 90 cents). Then he said the same thing again. I got more
nervous. He stopped smiling and looked at me strangely. He said
something different, I think. I didn't understand this either. Then I
noticed that there were people behind me in line, a lot of people.
They were all staring at me. They seemed to be in a hurry. They
wanted their donuts and coffee.

I took my coffee, left all the **change**, turned around, and walked
very quickly out of the shop. As I was going out the door, the
coffee cup hit the door **handle**. The cup dropped to the ground and
broke open. Hot coffee splashed everywhere. My legs were soaked
with hot coffee and cream. I was so embarrassed that I just ran
home. I even skipped going to the community college.

When I got home, I cried. I had tried hard to learn English, but
I couldn't understand anything. When my sister got home, I told
her what had happened. She laughed. She said, "The man in the
donut shop asked if you wanted anything else besides coffee. He
usually says, 'Anything else with that, **hon**?'" She also said, "He is

Latin: (generally)
Spanish-speaking
people

very friendly with all the **Latin** girls that come in. He likes to flirt more than he likes to sell donuts."

I will never forget that feeling. I was nervous and helpless. The man behind the counter was very nice, but his simple question confused me because I didn't expect it. I had practiced my questions too much. He probably thought I spoke English fluently. After this incident, I knew that I couldn't get by in English with just a few memorized phrases. I had to understand what other people said to me. I also learned that any situation in a second language can be difficult, even buying coffee.

What's the Story About?

Write short answers to these questions. Try to write *more* than one or two words.

1. Who tells this story? _____

   _____

2. Who does she live with? _____

   _____

3. Where does the action of this story *take place* (happen)? _____

   _____

4. What does the writer want to do when she goes out of the

   apartment? _____

   _____

5. Does she succeed in doing all these things? _____

   _____

6. What trouble does she have on this day? _____

   _____

7. Does she speak English as well as she needs to in order to "get

   by"? _____

   _____

8. What is the "real world"? _____

   _____

True or False

Are the following statements about the story true or false? Circle T (true) or F (false).

T   F   1. Evangelina's sister is not helpful to Evangelina.
T   F   2. Evangelina works as a waitress in a restaurant.
T   F   3. Evangelina's sister teaches Evangelina some expressions and phrases in English.
T   F   4. The man behind the counter at Joe's Donuts laughs at Evangelina.
T   F   5. This man understands everything Evangelina says.
T   F   6. This man is very nice.
T   F   7. Joe's Donuts is a popular place. It's always crowded with people.
T   F   8. Evangelina's sister has never been to Joe's Donuts.
T   F   9. Evangelina is a student at Bunker Hill Community College.
T   F   10. The people in line at Joe's Donuts are in a hurry.

Guessing Meaning

Guess the correct words from the following list to fill in the blanks. Use the right *form* of each word (verb, noun, adjective, or adverb) and use the right tense of verbs (past, present). The vocabulary comes from the story you have just read. However, the sentences are *not* about Evangelina's story. Other words in the sentence(s) give you clues to (help you guess) the meaning(s) of the missing word(s).

Verbs	*Nouns*	*Adjectives*	*Adverb*
flirt	expression	be in a hurry	fluently
get by	noise	common	
order	turn	helpless	
practice		nervous	
skip		popular	
splash		soaked	
stare			

1. I was very interested in the painting at the museum. I
   _____ at it for a long time.

2. I don't speak French _____, but I know enough to
   _____ _____ when I go to Paris. If I _____ it
   more, perhaps I would become fluent.

3. Carolina is afraid to speak English. When she has to speak it, she
   gets very _____ and can't think clearly.

4. Americans say "sure" a lot. It's a _____ (Adj)
   _____ (N) and it means "yes" or "okay."

5. The bakery was very busy. After I waited in line for 15 minutes,
   it was finally my _____. I _____ five croissants.

6. People in big cities always seem busy. They _____ _____
   _____ _____ to get somewhere else.

7. Monica likes Raul. She thinks that he's very attractive, very
   handsome. She _____ with him every day.

8. The child fell in the pool but was _____ because he
   couldn't swim.

9. The teenagers in the pool were very loud. The _____ was
   disturbing the neighbors.

10. The teacher dropped her coffee and it _____ on her.
    Her dress was _____.

11. Everyone likes Professor Kearns's history class. She is a
    _____ teacher. Students never _____ her
    classes. They go to all of them.

What Do You Think?

With a classmate or in small groups, discuss the following questions.

1. Describe your first "real world" experience with English.
2. Why was Evangelina embarrassed when she didn't understand the man in Joe's Donuts?
3. What are the most difficult situations in English for you? For example, talking on the phone, talking with a store clerk, talking with your teacher, and so on.
4. What English expressions did you learn first? (Or what functions did you learn—asking for something at the store or asking for someone on the phone?)

After discussing all of the questions, pick one of them to write about individually. Write your answer in one paragraph.

Key Words of the Story

Match the vocabulary words on the left with their meanings on the right. Write the word number on the line next to its meaning. (Dots (•) separate syllables. Stress marks (´) indicate the syllable stressed in pronunciation of the word.)

1. cóm•mon (Adj)

2. ex•prés•sion (N)

3. prác•tice (V)

4. ór•der (V)

5. get by (V)

6. póp•u•lar (Adj)

7. turn (N)

8. noise (N)

9. nér•vous (Adj)

10. stare (V)

11. be in a húr•ry (Adj)

12. splash (V)

13. soaked (Adj)

14. skip (V)

15. flirt (V)

16. hélp•less (Adj)

17. flú•ent•ly (Adv)

a. ___ a short saying; phrase

b. ___ to act playfully and romantically with someone

c. ___ to do something many times to improve

d. ___ not able to help oneself

e. ___ appearing or occurring frequently; not unusual

f. ___ with great ease; like a native speaker

g. ___ to not go; intentionally miss

h. ___ very wet

i. ___ liquid flying, such as when a full cup drops

j. ___ to request

k. ___ to look at intently

l. ___ to be very busy; to have no extra time

m. ___ to accomplish with minimal effort

n. ___ one's time to order or do something

o. ___ feeling uneasy; jumpy

p. ___ liked by many people

q. ___ annoying sound

Derived Forms

The table shows some vocabulary from chapter 5. Fill in the different forms of each word in the blank boxes. You can use an English-English (not a bilingual) dictionary. See page 9 in chapter 1 for more explanation.

Verb	Noun	Adjective	Adverb
		practiced	———
order		———	———
	terror		
		expressive	
———	popularity		
soak			———

Chapter 6
"For Here or To Go?"

Before You Read the Story

You can only learn to speak a language well when you *need* to speak it regularly. When you must use a new language to communicate about basic matters, such as the need to eat, the new language suddenly becomes very important. Constant and realistic practice in everyday situations is better than any grammar exercise. José, who is from Venezuela, learns this lesson during his first stay in the United States. Look carefully at the drawings with the story on the following pages. Can you "read" the story in these drawings?

• • • • • • • • • • • • • • • •

"For Here or To Go?"

I used to think that English was easy. I studied it in Venezuela for two years, though I never studied it very hard. My English teacher was Venezuelan. She spoke Spanish with us most of the time. We didn't practice English outside of class because we never had the opportunity or the need. Our teacher never *made* us speak it outside of class. I guess I didn't learn to speak English well in Venezuela because I never *needed* to speak it there.

Mostly, I remember phrases from class and some slang expressions from friends. My favorite American expression was "money talks." It means that money does anything. It works for you. Why

study English, I thought, when my money would **"talk"** for me? Dollars speak English in the U.S., **bolivars** speak Spanish in Venezuela, **yen** speak Japanese in Japan, etc.

In my last year of high school, my parents sent me to the U.S. for a year as a **foreign exchange student**. Suddenly, I *needed* to speak English. I lived with a very nice American family, my **host family**, in their home. The parents lived in a small city in northern Arizona called Flagstaff. The couple had one daughter, who was a student at the university. They had lived in Spain for a year a long time before, and their daughter was studying Spanish in college, so we spoke Spanish at home. I think they wanted a Spanish-speaking exchange student to practice their Spanish. That was okay with me. I was relieved not to have to speak English with them right away—or at any time.

School didn't start for another week. I had some free time. A few days after I had arrived, I left the house on my own to explore the town. It was eleven o'clock in the morning, and the family had already eaten breakfast. Americans have their meals too early for me. I missed breakfast and was too hungry to wait for lunch.

When I saw a McDonald's restaurant in town, I thought I could order something to eat there without trouble. By "trouble," I mean

"talk": Talk is in quotes here because it is a figurative use; money can't actually talk.

bolivar: the unit of currency (money) in Venezuela

yen: the unit of currency in Japan

foreign exchange student: a student who lives and studies in another country, usually for one year

host family: a family that a foreign exchange student lives with

fast food: food that you can get quickly at restaurants such as McDonald's, Burger King, etc.

register: the machine in a store that adds up—or registers— the sale amount and holds the cash

shrug: to raise the shoulders in doubt

heat lamp: light placed over food to keep it warm

English. After all, I had been in the U.S. for three days and I hadn't spoken much English. I wasn't ready to start speaking it then. I just wanted something to eat. I thought I could simply order the same things here that I order at the McDonald's back home in Venezuela.

I walked in and saw that they were very busy. Americans must love **fast food**. While I waited in line, I studied the large menu. When it was my turn to order, I said, "Big Mac, Coke, large fries, please." The man behind the counter told me how much it cost, but I didn't understand him. I looked at the **register** to see the amount in numbers. Then he said something else that I didn't understand at all: "For here or to go?" I **shrugged** my shoulders, and he repeated, "For here or to go?" I didn't know what to say, so I just said, "No, thank you."

The man gave me the Coke and the french fries but not the Big Mac. Instead, he explained something to me and pointed to where all the hamburgers, except the Big Macs, were piling up under the **heat lamps**. I didn't understand a word he said, but I thought maybe he was talking about the problem with the Big Macs. Then

mine: here it means my order

keep an eye on (idiom): to watch carefully

he started to take the orders of other people, and I thought he had forgotten about **mine**. I took my Coke and french fries to a table and **kept an eye on** the man. I thought he would call me when the cooks made more Big Macs, but he didn't. In fact, I saw him giving other customers their Big Macs. So where was mine? I became upset. Did he just forget, or did he not like me because I couldn't understand him? In any case, I was helpless because I couldn't explain my problem to him and wouldn't have understood his answer anyway.

When there was no one else in line, I walked up to the counter and said to the same man, "Excuse me. I ordered a Big Mac." He entered the cost of another Big Mac on the register. He didn't remember me or my first Big Mac at all! Rather than try to explain my story to him, I said, "No, thank you" again and walked out. On the way home I thought about how a Big Mac in America might be the same as a Big Mac in Venezuela but ordering it here was different. My money didn't "talk" after all.

When I got home, I felt foolish. I told my host family about my experience. They explained that the man at McDonald's had said, "For here or to go?" which means "Would you like to eat in this

restaurant, or would you like to take the food home?" Workers in fast food restaurants always ask customers this question. But what happened to my Big Mac? My host family thought that maybe the worker forgot that I was waiting for one. He needed me to remind him, but my English wasn't good enough to remind him that I had already paid for a Big Mac and was waiting for it.

I still felt foolish. Here I was in America, but I couldn't, or didn't, speak English. I decided to start using the English that I did know. When I first started to speak English with the family, they were a little surprised. At first I spoke mostly Spanish with a little English. Later, I could speak mostly English with a few Spanish words. The family didn't correct my English, so I felt at ease speaking it around them. It wasn't very good English at first, but I knew it got better every day with practice. My English *had to* improve—or I'd starve.

What's the Story About?

Write short answers to these questions. Try to write *more* than one or two words.

1. Why was José in the United States? _____

   _____

2. Who did he live with? _____

   _____

3. Did he like who he lived with? How do you know this? _____

   _____

4. Why did José go out on his own a few days after he arrived in

   Flagstaff? _____

   _____

5. Why did José become upset? _____

   _____

6. Did his attitude toward learning English change? If so, how?

_____

7. Did his attitude toward Big Macs change? If so, how? _____

_____

8. José's English teacher in Venezuela spoke Spanish. Should language teachers be native speakers? Should they use the students' first language to teach? _____

_____

_____

True or False

Are the following statements about the story true or false? Circle T (true) or F (false).

T   F   1. José studied English seriously so that he could earn more money someday.

T   F   2. José didn't need to speak English in Venezuela.

T   F   3. José knew a foreign exchange student from Japan.

T   F   4. José's host family spoke Spanish at home.

T   F   5. José ordered his food in Spanish at the McDonald's.

T   F   6. "For here or to go?" is a polite greeting.

T   F   7. The man who took José's order kept an eye on him.

T   F   8. José finally decided to start practicing his English with the family.

Guessing Meaning

Guess the correct words from the following list to fill in the blanks. Use the right *form* of each word (verb, noun, adjective, or adverb) and use the right tense of verbs (past, present). The vocabulary comes from the story you have just read. However, the sentences are *not* about José's story. Other words in the sentence(s) give you clues to (help you guess) the meaning(s) of the missing word(s).

Verbs	*Nouns*	*Adjectives*	*Adverb*
make	couple	at ease	right away
miss	free time	busy	
pile	opportunity	slang	
point	phrase	upset	
remind	trouble		
starve			

1. The teacher _____ to the chalkboard and said, "Answer these questions." She _____ the students write an essay for each question, though they didn't want to.

2. We have to pay rent tomorrow. Can you _____ me to write a check? Otherwise, I'll forget.

3. Do you have any _____ _____ this afternoon, or are you _____?

4. Tom learned several short _____ in Spanish before he went to Mexico. But he had some _____ understanding the people there because they used a lot of _____ expressions that he didn't understand.

5. I hope I have an _____ to see my parents this Christmas. If not, they will be very _____. They haven't seen me in two years.

6. Yuki is no longer nervous and uncomfortable in her English class.

   She seems _____ _____ with her classmates.

7. The young _____ had two children.

8. The teacher was sick again today. He _____ class.

9. Tim has too many books. He _____ them all on top of his

   desk.

10. I haven't eaten all day. If I don't eat something _____

    _____, I'll _____!

What Do You Think?

With a classmate or in small groups, discuss the following questions.

1. How did José's attitude toward learning English change? How will
   this help him or hurt him during his stay in Flagstaff?
2. Have you ever been helpless because you couldn't speak English?
   If so, describe the situation.
3. Imagine that you were in José's place in the McDonald's restaurant. How would you have communicated with the man behind
   the counter without knowing much English?

After discussing all of the questions, pick one of them to write about
individually. Write your answer in one paragraph.

Key Words of the Story

Match the vocabulary words on the left with their meanings on the right. Write the word number on the line next to its meaning. (Dots (•) separate syllables. Stress marks (ʹ) indicate the syllable stressed in pronunciation of the word.)

1. op•por•tú•ni•ty (N)

2. make (V)

3. phrase (N)

4. slang (Adj)

5. cóu•ple (N)

6. right a•wáy (Adv)

7. free time (N)

8. miss (V)

9. tróu•ble (N)

10. bús•y (Adj)

11. point (V)

12. pile (V)

13. up•sét (Adj)

14. re•mínd (V)

15. at ease (Adj)

16. starve (V)

a. ____ a husband and wife or boyfriend and girlfriend (or, generally, two of anything)

b. ____ informal language

c. ____ immediately; without waiting

d. ____ an expression; a group of words

e. ____ comfortable; not under stress or pressure

f. ____ to be without food and very hungry

g. ____ time not working; leisure time

h. ____ to force or require

i. ____ chance

j. ____ to fail to do or attend

k. ____ problem; difficulty

l. ____ having a lot to do, much activity

m. ____ to say again or make someone remember

n. ____ angry; bothered

o. ____ to place one thing on top of another

p. ____ to put one's finger toward something to show someone

Derived Forms

The table shows some vocabulary from chapter 6. Fill in the different forms of each word in the blank boxes. You can use an English-English (not a bilingual) dictionary. See page 9 in chapter 1 for more explanation.

Verb	Noun	Adjective	Adverb
connect		connected/connecting	
		piled	————
	reminder	————	————
	starvation		————
			necessarily
	upset		————

Chapter 7
"I'll Say What I Want"

Before You Read the Story

As beginners, second language students are often afraid of speaking the new language. They feel especially intimidated in front of native speakers of the language. Wedyah, who is from Riyadh, Saudi Arabia, has a different problem. She finds Americans very friendly and easy to talk to. But some of her **countrymen** studying with her are not as pleased with her. Look carefully at the drawings with the story on the following pages. Can you "read" the story in these drawings?

countrymen: other people from the same country; here, from Saudi Arabia

nightclub: disco; bar where people dance

• • • • • • • • • • • • • • •

"I'll Say What I Want"

I want to tell this story because I'm frustrated. I'm frustrated by some of my classmates. My English has become very good, but certain people in class think that I should not use it, that I should not speak as much as I do. I think they're wrong.

For almost two years I've been studying in an intensive English language program at an American university. I've made many friends here, especially American friends. My American ESL teachers have been very interesting and friendly. I often talk to them after class or when I see them on campus. My video lab teacher is especially cute and nice. He has told me about good restaurants and **nightclubs** in town.

My best friend works in the English program office. I should say that she is my best *American* friend, since I have friends back home in Riyadh. She is learning Arabic, so we have become **conversation partners**. Sometimes we speak in Arabic, sometimes in English.

conversation partner: someone to talk to in order to practice a foreign language

My daily interaction with these Americans has greatly improved my English. In Arabic, I'm very talkative. And now in English I can be talkative, or outgoing, too. I think that I am well prepared to study at an American college. I want to go to a school of nursing so that I can return home and work as a nurse.

Well, you might think that everything sounds great. It *is* great. I really enjoy my life studying in America. It's wonderful. But I have one little problem in some of my classes. I cannot call it a serious problem, but it does frustrate me.

I'm from Saudi Arabia, which is a very conservative Muslim country. Men and women behave very differently in my culture, especially in public. In a group of men, a woman's opinion is not respected. In many public situations, in fact, women are not supposed to express their opinions. This is not true in America. Here, I want to express myself freely. I want to say what I think because I am as smart as any man. I believed that I could express myself here and not worry about restrictions of my speech.

In my classes, sometimes male students from Arab countries do not like my opinions. Not *all* male Arab students react this way, but some do, especially conservative ones from my country, Saudi Arabia. Actually, they don't like it when I express my opinion at all. They think that I should sit and be quiet, that I should listen to the teacher and to the male students in the class. They become annoyed when I speak up often. Sometimes when I speak up in class they laugh or look down and close their eyes. Sometimes they talk to another classmate or tell the teacher a different answer. Most of the time, though, they disagree with me and say, "No. You're wrong." They don't want to have a discussion with me, but they want to say in front of the class, "No, you're wrong." I tell these students, "Listen, I'll say what I want. I **have a mind of my own.**" I think that these men become the most annoyed when the teacher says, "Yes, Wedyah, very good," or, "That's an excellent point, Wedyah."

I annoy some of these men because of other things that I do, too. I often go out to nightclubs with my American friends and drink **cocktails**. I dress the way my American friends dress, which reveals more of my body and my skin than traditional Muslim dress does. I also drive a car here. It is *illegal* for women to drive a car in most of my country.

have a mind of one's own: an expression meaning "I can think for myself and have my own opinions"

cocktail: alcoholic beverage; liquor

I know that I annoy some of these male Arab students. This is our culture. They are not used to women speaking up or doing many other things. It's difficult for them to listen to me. But I don't care. As long as I'm in America, I'll speak up and do the things that my American friends do. And as long as these Arab students are in America also, they will have to get used to me and other women.

What's the Story About?

Write short answers to these questions. Try to write *more* than one or two words.

1. What is Wedyah's occupation (i.e., what is she doing now)? _____

   _____

2. What are her future plans? _____

   _____

3. Does she speak English well? How do you know? _____

_____

4. Does she enjoy studying English? _____

_____

5. Where does she use English? With whom? _____

_____

6. What is frustrating her? _____

_____

7. What is her personality like (i.e., what kind of person is she)?

_____

8. Does she act more like an American or a Saudi woman? Why?

_____

True or False

Are the following statements about the story true or false? Circle T (true) or F (false).

T   F   1. Wedyah is not a very conservative man.
T   F   2. She has trouble with one of her ESL teachers.
T   F   3. Her conversation partner is an American learning Arabic.
T   F   4. Wedyah is talkative and outgoing.
T   F   5. She is worried about expressing her opinion in front of American men.
T   F   6. Her teacher drinks cocktails in class and wears revealing clothes.
T   F   7. Wedyah thinks that one of her Arab classmates is cute.
T   F   8. Her lifestyle in the United States is different in many ways from her life in Saudi Arabia.

Guessing Meaning

Guess the correct words from the following list to fill in the blanks. Use the right *form* of each word (verb, noun, or adjective) and use the right tense of verbs (past, present). The vocabulary comes from the story you have just read. However, the sentences are *not* about Wedyah's story. Other words in the sentence(s) give you clues to (help you guess) the meaning(s) of the missing word(s).

Verbs	**Nouns**	**Adjectives**
be supposed to	campus	annoyed
be used to	interaction	conservative
express	restriction	cute
react		frustrated
		intensive
		outgoing
		talkative

1. Jill is a very _____ and _____ student. She likes to _____ her opinions at school and go to parties. She is especially talkative with _____ men that she likes.

2. When I went to France, I took an _____ French language program at the Sorbonne. It was a short program, but I had to study very hard.

3. My mother becomes _____ when people start to smoke near her. Sometimes she asks them to stop smoking and they _____ very defensively. When they do not stop smoking, she becomes _____.

4. Harvard University has a beautiful _____ in Cambridge, Massachusetts. The center of it is called "Harvard Yard."

5. In some very _____ cultures, _____

between unmarried men and women is not allowed. In America

and most European countries, however, men and women work,

play, and socialize with each other regularly. There are few

_____ on their relationships.

6. In most American classrooms, students _____ _____

_____ speak up and express their opinions. Japan is differ-

ent. There, most students _____ _____ _____

sitting quietly and listening to the teacher instead of participat-

ing.

What Do You Think?

With a classmate or in small groups, discuss the following questions.

1. How do you think you and your countrymen are different from
   Americans?
2. In your English classes, do you see some students becoming
   Americanized (i.e., more like Americans)?
3. How are men and women different in your country? For example, are women restricted from driving or serving in the military or politics?
4. How do you feel about Wedyah's behavior? In America, should
   she behave as an American or as a Saudi woman?

After discussing all of the questions, pick one of them to write about individually. Write your answer in one paragraph.

Key Words of the Story

Match the vocabulary words on the left with their meanings on the right. Write the word number on the line next to its meaning. (Dots (•) separate syllables. Stress marks (´) indicate the syllable stressed in pronunciation of the word.)

1. frús•trat•ed (Adj)

2. in•tén•sive (Adj)

3. cám•pus (N)

4. cute (Adj)

5. in•ter•ác•tion (N)

6. tálk•a•tive (Adj)

7. out•gó•ing (Adj)

8. con•sér•va•tive (Adj)

9. be sup•pósed to (V)

10. ex•préss (V)

a. ____ the buildings and grounds of a school

b. ____ upset or bothered by something or someone

c. ____ knowing something by habit; accustomed to or familiar with something

d. ____ energetic and sociable

e. ____ do not like or accept change easily

f. ____ must; to be required to

11. re•stríc•tion (N)

12. re•áct (V)

13. an•nóyed (Adj)

14. used to (Adj)

g. ___ to say to others

h. ___ limit

i. ___ to respond to something said or done

j. ___ upset and discouraged by something you cannot change

k. ___ comprehensive; concentrated; requiring much attention and work

l. ___ talk or involvement with others

m. ___ to enjoy talking a lot

n. ___ attractive appearance

Derived Forms

The table shows some vocabulary from chapter 7. Fill in the different forms of each word in the blank boxes. You can use an English-English (not a bilingual) dictionary. See page 9 in chapter 1 for more explanation.

Verb	Noun	Adjective	Adverb
	intensity		
restrict			———
	frustration		
receive		receptive	
	annoyance		

Part 3. Understanding a New People

• • • • • • • • • • • • • • • • • • • •

Chapter 8
Time to Relax

 ## Before You Read the Story

Carlos, from Buenos Aires, Argentina, is trying to understand how Americans think about time. He thinks they rush too much—or more than most Spanish speakers, anyway. They are too concerned with time and being **punctual**. Look carefully at the drawings with the story on the following pages. Can you "read" the story in these drawings?

• • • • • • • • • • • • • • •

Time to Relax

People from different cultures think about time in different ways. But how is this possible? There are 24 hours in the day everywhere, in every country. How can time be different? It is.

I attend Boston University. One-third of the students who attend this school are international students. They come from all over the world, many of them from **Latin America**. There is a large, comfortable **cafeteria** on campus. I go there every day during school with my friends. Many of them are from Latin America and Spain. **For the most part**, the American students eat lunch in the cafeteria between noon and two o'clock. I rarely see any of them stay for more than an hour. They get their food and eat as quickly as they can. When they leave, the cafeteria is still full of Latinos. The Latinos linger for several hours talking, laughing, smoking, and drinking soda and coffee. Sometimes their lunch goes until four o'clock. They stay as long as their friends stay. They don't leave because they have to do something else. I think that there are

punctual: on time; not late

Latin America: countries of South and Central America

cafeteria: large room where meals for many people are served

for the most part: generally; mostly

71

also a lot of Arab students there. They seem to take more time to eat and talk as well.

I think the Latinos stay longer for three reasons. First, they are used to eating their breakfast, lunch, and dinner later in the day than Americans eat theirs. Second, they are used to taking more time at each meal, eating slowly and leisurely. They don't eat more food; they just take more time. Third, I think that family and friends are more important to Spanish speakers than school or **careers**. They would rather relax and talk to their friends during a meal than **rush off** to study or work. Maybe this is not true everywhere, but I think it is true here at Boston University.

The American students, on the other hand, are just the opposite. They come to the cafeteria only to eat. They don't stay and talk for very long. When they have something else to do, they leave, even when their friends are still at the table. When they get up from the table to leave, it seems they always look at their watches first. They often say something such as "Whoa, look at the time! I have to go." Then they run off. They would rather obey their watches than stay with their friends.

I noticed many peculiar things about American eating habits actually. I mentioned only their habit of rushing through a meal,

career: a lifelong job; profession

rush off: to leave in a hurry

cellular: wireless phone carried in the pocket or in a car

but there are other peculiar practices. For example, they eat everywhere. I've seen people eating in their cars while they are driving. I've seen people eating *and* talking on a **cellular** phone while they're driving! On campus, I see students and teachers walking while drinking coffee or eating a sandwich. I think these habits are all related to time. They don't want to "waste" time eating. They have to accomplish something else while they eat, such as walking somewhere, or driving, or studying, or reading the newspaper, or watching TV. An American friend told me that most American families don't usually eat meals in their dining rooms. They eat in the living room while watching TV.

So you can see why I believe that Americans are obsessed with time. All of the Americans I know have wristwatches, but many of my Latino friends don't regularly wear one. I don't. Americans are always setting their watches, making sure the time is "exact." I once heard two American students arguing about what time it was. One said, "It's 3:45." The other said, "No it's not! It's 3:48, you idiot!" But that's how Americans think about time. It's the most important thing in their lives.

People do think about time differently after all. It seems to me, though, that the American and Latino students do everything they're supposed to do. They work and study about the same amount. But the Latinos don't feel as pressured by time as the Americans do. It's no **wonder** that Americans are so stressed out.

wonder: surprise

What's the Story About?

Write short answers to these questions. Try to write *more* than one or two words.

1. What is Carlos trying to figure out? _____

   _____

2. Who are Carlos's friends? _____

   _____

3. How do the Latinos spend their lunchtime? _____

   _____

4. How do the American students spend their lunchtime? _____

_____

5. Why do the Latinos stay in the cafeteria longer? _____

_____

6. How do the Americans think about time? _____

_____

7. When do the American students end their lunchtime? _____

_____

8. In what peculiar ways do Americans sometimes eat their meals?

_____

 ## True or False

Are the following statements about the story true or false? Circle T (true) or F (false).

T   F   1. Carlos is from Latin America.
T   F   2. American students get more things done than Latinos do.
T   F   3. Many students at Boston University are from Latin America.
T   F   4. The cafeteria is empty at 2:00 in the afternoon.
T   F   5. Many of the Latinos linger in the cafeteria until 4:00.
T   F   6. Carlos takes 24 hours to eat lunch.
T   F   7. Carlos once heard two students arguing over the exact time.
T   F   8. Carlos thinks that Americans obey their watches.
T   F   9. Americans are less stressed out by time than Latinos are.
T   F   10. Time is very important to Americans.

Guessing Meaning

Guess the correct words from the following list to fill in the blanks. Use the right *form* of each word (verb, noun, adjective, or adverb) and use the right tense of verbs (past, present). The vocabulary comes from the story you have just read. However, the sentences are *not* about Carlos's story. Other words in the sentence(s) give you clues to (help you guess) the meanings of the missing word(s).

Verbs	*Noun*	*Adjectives*	*Adverbs*
accomplish	habit	obsessed	leisurely
attend		peculiar	rarely
linger		related to	
obey		stressed out	
relax			
rush			
take time			

1. Some people like to spend a lot of time eating. They

   _____ at the table long after they finish and don't

   _____ to do something else.

2. Mary Ann doesn't like the college cafeteria. She _____

   eats there. She eats at Café Paradiso, instead, where she can eat

   slowly and _____ in the quiet surroundings.

3. Linda has the _____(Adj) _____ (N) of

   eating pizza and drinking soda for breakfast. Normally, people

   have coffee and cereal or bread for breakfast.

4. I don't like tests. I get very _____ _____ during

   final exams week when I have four or five exams to take.

5. Not many children do everything their parents tell them to do.

Not many _____ their parents' every wish.

6. Rob works at his computer constantly. He thinks about nothing

else. He might even be _____ with it.

7. We had a very busy day today. We didn't have time to

_____ at all. Fortunately, we _____ a lot.

We got all our work done.

8. You have to be very careful when you paint. Don't rush;

_____ your _____.

9. Teaching English as a second language is _____

_____ the field of linguistics. Most ESL teachers study

linguistics in college.

10. I went to Smith College in Northampton, Massachusetts. What

college did you _____?

What Do You Think?

With a classmate or in small groups, discuss the following questions.

1. How do you think about time? Do you act more like Carlos or the American students that Carlos describes?
2. Do you agree with Carlos that Americans "obey" their watches? Explain why or why not.
3. Make two lists: one list of countries, such as America, that obey their watches and another list of countries that are more relaxed about time. Discuss any patterns in your lists.
4. Should people eat their meals at the dinner table? What is a proper or appropriate meal? For example, in Spain, it is rude to eat or drink in the car. Their cars do not have "cup holders"—special places to hold drinks while people are driving.

After discussing all of the questions, pick one of them to write about individually. Write your answer in about three paragraphs.

Key Words of the Story

Match the vocabulary words on the left with their meanings on the right. Write the word number on the line next to its meaning. (Dots (•) separate syllables. Stress marks (´) indicate the syllable stressed in pronunciation of the word.)

1. fíg•ure out (V)
2. rush (V)
3. at•ténd (V)
4. ráre•ly (Adv)
5. lín•ger (V)
6. take time (V)
7. léi•sure•ly (Adv)
8. re•láx (V)
9. o•béy (V)
10. pe•cú•liar (Adj)
11. háb•it (N)
12. re•lát•ed (Adj)
13. ac•cóm•plish (V)
14. ob•séssed (Adj)
15. stressed out (Adj)

a. ___ to stay longer or be slow in leaving

b. ___ to do something slowly, carefully

c. ___ feeling too much pressure, anxiety; nervous

d. ___ very concerned with; thinking too much about one thing or person

e. ___ slowly; at a comfortable pace

f. ___ to do successfully; to complete

g. ___ to rest; to make less nervous or stressed

h. ___ connected to; having a relationship with

i. ___ very seldom; hardly ever; almost never

j. ___ to go to

k. ___ a usual, customary activity done regularly

l. ___ different; strange; odd

m. ___ to do things quickly

n. ___ to behave as directed by someone or something (such as a clock)

o. ___ to try to understand

Derived Forms

The table shows some vocabulary from chapter 8. Fill in the different forms of each word in the blank boxes. You can use an English-English (not a bilingual) dictionary. See page 9 in chapter 1 for more explanation.

Verb	Noun	Adjective	Adverb
	relaxation		
		attending	————
obsess			
	accomplishment		————
————	habit		
————			peculiarly

Chapter 9
Our Parents' Goals

Before You Read the Story

Suzy grew up in the United States. Her parents, however, grew up in China and are not as familiar with American ways as their daughter is. We say that Suzy is "Chinese American." She is an American whose family came from China. Because they grew up in different cultures, Suzy and her parents have different views on education. Look carefully at the drawings with the story on the following pages. Can you "read" the story in these drawings?

. . . .

Our Parents' Goals

I am a Chinese American college student. I was born in the United States, but my parents came to this country shortly before I was born. They grew up in China. At home, I learned Chinese and did not learn English until I started school. English feels like my **native** language now, so I don't have any problems with it. In fact, I have more problems with Chinese. Only my parents and older family members speak to me in Chinese. I say that my English is better than my Chinese because I never used Chinese at school. In Chinese, I can say simple things, but in English I can say **complex** things. I think I sound like a child when I speak Chinese.

My parents own a business here and work very hard. They rarely relax or take vacations. They say they are making sacrifices

native: here it means first

complex: sophisticated; having many ideas

for me so that I can have a good life in America. They tell me all the time, "You have many more opportunities here than we had in China." They expect me to work as hard in school as they work in their business. They are still more Chinese than American. They went to school in China and only learned simple English here in America. Their friends and most of their customers are Chinese, too. My parents pressure me to excel at school work more than most American parents do. I wish they understood more about American culture.

When I was in **elementary school**, my parents expected me to come home immediately after school to study. As soon as I came in the house, my parents sent me to my room to study until dinner. Then, after dinner, I returned to studying until bedtime. I studied like this almost every day, even when I didn't have any homework. I could watch television or play games with my friends only on Saturdays. Sundays were "family days," so I helped prepare the large Sunday meal at home with my parents, brothers, aunts, uncles, and some cousins. The Sunday meal was a big, important event, and I couldn't miss it.

In high school, when my American friends were dating, my parents wouldn't allow me to **date** boys. They said I was not old

elementary school: grades 1 through 5 or 8 (ages 5 to 12), sometimes called "grammar school"

date: to be romantic friends (as a girlfriend or boyfriend)

part-time job:
work after school or
on weekends, not
full time

scholarship: an
award of money to
pay for college

pay off: to benefit
or reward
[someone]

medical school:
school after college
to train to become a
doctor

enough to date and that I should be studying instead. When other kids were getting **part-time jobs** after school and buying cars, my parents said that studying was more important than buying a car or other "frivolous" things.

My American friends, on the other hand, stayed outside and played or watched television after school. Their parents did not order them to study in their rooms every day. Usually, their parents were not even at home in the afternoon, so the kids were free to do whatever they wanted. The only time they had to study was after dinner, but they only studied when they had homework. They dated and had part-time jobs to pay for cars, motorcycles, clothes, or anything else they wanted.

My parents expected that I would never fail in school. I had to compete in every academic competition, such as essay contests or science fairs, so that I would win a **scholarship** to college. When I did win a scholarship, my parents told me that my studying had **paid off**.

Now that I am in college, I have to work as hard as I ever worked before. My parents want me to keep my scholarship and get into the best **medical school** after college. I still have no time to relax with my friends during the school year. In the summers, while other students are on vacation at the beach or working at fun jobs, I am still in summer school. Sometimes I get depressed. I need more variety in my activities.

I know many Asian American students like me. Our parents do not allow us to fail or be average. We must achieve the goals that our parents set for us. We must feel thankful for the opportunity that we have and not "waste" time playing games or sports, dating, or buying cars. These parents do not understand American culture. They did not go to school here, and they usually do not understand English as well as their children do. They do not realize that America is very different from China, Korea, Japan, or other Asian countries. They do not understand that in American education, studying is not always the most important part of school. Sports and social and other **extracurricular activities** are as important as studying. They say to their children, "Study! You must study hard to succeed. You have many more opportunities here than we had back home."

Consequently, some Asian American students feel frustrated. Their parents pressure them too much to excel. They feel they are living their parents' lives, not their own lives. Some of our American friends tell us to say to our parents, "I don't care if I don't get an

extracurricular activities: school activities other than classes, e.g., sports, clubs

A on every test." But we cannot say this to our parents. Most Chinese parents would not tolerate such disrespect. We must do what our parents say, or we are being disrespectful.

Someday, I would like to help my children achieve *their* goals. I hope that they are successful, but I will not prevent them from playing, having fun, and being like their friends sometimes. I will also respect *their* choices. I will help them decide on a career, but I don't think that I will pressure them to become doctors, as my parents pressured me. In this way, I think I will combine the best of Asian *and* American cultures in my children's upbringing. I will teach them to work hard, respect their family, and choose their own careers.

What's the Story About?

Write short answers to these questions. Try to write *more* than one or two words.

1. What is Suzy's occupation now? _____

   _____

2. What is her nationality? _____

   _____

3. Where are her parents from? _____

   _____

4. What do her parents pressure her to do? _____

   _____

5. How does she feel about this? _____

   _____

6. How much time does Suzy spend with her friends? _____

   _____

7. How is Suzy like other Asian American students? _____

_____

8. How will Suzy raise her children? Will this be different from her

own upbringing? _____

_____

Using the Best Word

Circle the best word to complete each sentence. The vocabulary
comes from the story you have just read. However, the sentences are
not about Suzy's story.

Verbs	*Nouns*	*Adjectives*
achieve	sacrifice	depressed
compete	variety	familiar
excel at	view	frivolous
fail		
pressure		
set		
tolerate		

1. Linda never wastes time with *upbringing / frivolous / depressed*
   activities such as watching TV or playing with dolls. She studies
   most of the time and excels at school.
2. My parents *pressured / compete / fail* me to study hard in college.
   They didn't want me to fail.
3. In most American stores, there is a great *variety / sacrifice /
   complex* of products. Customers have many choices.
4. Have you *set / achieved / paid off* the goals that your parents set
   for you?
5. Some people become *familiar / frivolous / depressed* when it rains.
6. I don't smoke and can't *achieve / sacrifice / tolerate* other people
   smoking around me, especially in restaurants. My *disrespect /
   view / experience* is that people should be restricted from smoking
   in restaurants.

7. I've been to France many times. I'm *set / depressed / familiar* with many French habits.
8. If you want to achieve any goal, you must make certain *native / scholarships / sacrifices*. For example, you might have to skip expensive vacations to save money to buy a house. Otherwise, you shouldn't *set / tolerate / fail* such high goals.
9. Usually, people who *familiar / sacrifice / excel at* sports like to *set / compete / view*.
10. Someone who is very competitive doesn't like to *fail / achieve / compete*.

What Do You Think?

With a classmate or in small groups, discuss the following questions.

1. What is the tone of Suzy's story? That is, is she happy? angry? content? Explain.
2. How does Suzy say she wants to raise her children? Is this the same as her upbringing?

Finish the Story
3. Imagine that you are in Suzy's situation. Would you accept the goals that your parents set for you? Would you rebel against (not accept) what your parents wanted you to do? Rewrite the end of this story (the last paragraph) in your own words.

After discussing all of the questions, pick one of them to write about individually. Write your answer in about three paragraphs.

Key Words of the Story

Match the vocabulary words on the left with their meanings on the right. Write the word number on the line next to its meaning. (Dots (•) separate syllables. Stress marks (ʹ) indicate the syllable stressed in pronunciation of the word.)

1. fa•míl•iar (Adj)   a. ___ to reach and accomplish a goal

2. view (N)   b. ___ something given up or offered

3. sác•ri•fice (N)   c. ___ to decide on something (such as a goal)

4. prés•sure (V)

5. ex•cél at (V)   d. ___ used to something or known

6. frív•o•lous (Adj)   e. ___ to strongly encourage; to force

7. fail (V)   f. ___ an assortment; different sorts or types

8. com•péte (V)   g. ___ perspective; idea; thought

9. de•préssed (Adj)   h. ___ to struggle to win against others

10. va•rí•e•ty (N)   i. ___ to not excel or succeed

11. a•chíeve (V)   j. ___ to endure; to accept without liking; to
                            put up with
12. set (V)

13. tól•er•ate (V)   k. ___ very sad; dejected

                        l. ___ to do very well

                        m. ___ silly and unnecessary

Derived Forms

The table shows some vocabulary from chapter 9. Fill in the different
forms of each word in the blank boxes. You can use an English-
English (not a bilingual) dictionary. See page 9 in chapter 1 for more
explanation.

Verb	Noun	Adjective	Adverb
		excellent	
	failure		
		competitive	
tolerate			
			depressingly
		sacrificial	

Chapter 10
Like Having an Old Car

Before You Read the Story

When he first arrives in the United States, Thierry, from Grenoble, France, doesn't understand Americans. He judges their actions from a French perspective. He therefore **misunderstands** how American friends treat each other. Look carefully at the drawings with the story on the following pages. Can you "read" the story in these drawings?

• • • • • • • • • • • • • • •

Like Having an Old Car

I come from Grenoble, France. I'm now a college **senior** in Chicago. My father, who works for an American company back home in Grenoble, also went to college in the United States. He always wanted me to go to college here. He thought English fluency and an American college degree would be good for my career because they were good for his career. He thinks that I will get a better job in France as well.

Although I had studied English for many years, I never really wanted to go to college in America. I had heard that American schools weren't as good as French schools. Besides, I didn't want to leave my friends (especially my girlfriend) in Grenoble. Nonetheless, after *lycée* (French high school) I began college at a university in Chicago.

Chicago is a very large American city. There are many manufacturing companies around Chicago. The jobs at many of those

misunderstand: to not understand

senior: each year in high school or college has a name:
  freshman: first year
  sophomore: second year
  junior: third year
  senior: fourth year

companies are called "blue collar" jobs. A blue collar job requires manual labor but not a college degree. College-educated professionals have "white collar" jobs. Americans sometimes call Chicago the city with "big shoulders." I think it got that **nickname** from its large blue collar workforce. **Manual labor** makes people strong and tough, giving them big shoulders. At least that's how I think the city got its nickname. In any case, the people here are **proud**, tough, and **self sufficient**. People also call Chicago the "windy city" because of the wind that blows from Lake Michigan.

At first, I liked Chicago. It was very different from Grenoble— much bigger, noisier, and exciting. Grenoble is a small city in the French Alps. It is a beautiful city with skiing and many historical sites nearby. It's also cleaner and much safer than Chicago, but sometimes it's boring.

When I first arrived in Chicago to start college, I met many people. The Americans were very friendly and helpful. I thought that they cared about me in ways that the French, unless they know you very well, don't care. People always greeted me by saying, "Hi, Thierry! How are you?" They often invited me to their homes and apartments for lunch or dinner or to watch television. In France, friends usually don't go to each other's homes. Instead,

nickname: a short, familiar name that your friends and family call you

manual labor: physical work; work with hands

proud: feeling very pleased with oneself; feeling superior

self-sufficient: provide for oneself without relying on others

they go to a café or some other public place. I enjoyed seeing how Americans socialize. And my English improved very quickly this way.

After about a month, however, I began to realize that these Americans didn't really care about me. They asked me, "How are you doing?" every time they saw me, but they didn't really mean it. They either didn't care or didn't have the time to listen to me. They were more interested in their obligations, the things they had to do. They always seemed to be in a rush to go somewhere else or to do something else.

I started to think that the common American greeting "How are you doing?" was merely another way of saying "Hi." It was not a sincere question about someone's well-being. If an American says, "How are you doing?" he doesn't want you to give him an honest answer. He expects you to say, "Fine. **And you?**"

So I decided to experiment with these Americans. I wanted to know how sincere they really were. At lunch time one day I passed a classmate in the cafeteria. He said, "Hi, Thierry! How are you doing?" I said, "Oh, not good, Eric." Then he said, "Okay, **see you around**," and continued walking away.

The same thing happened the next day with a different class-mate. When I saw her in the hallway, she said, "**Hey**, Thierry!

"And you?": "And how are you doing?"

"See you around" (informal expression): "I'll see you later"

"Hey" (informal expression): "Hi"

"What's up?"
(informal
expression): "What
have you been
doing these days?"

insincere: not
sincere or caring

pizzeria: a
restaurant that
makes pizzas

What's up?" I said, "Hi, Stephanie. Actually, I'm not doing well."
She smiled and said, "Oh, sorry. Talk to you later." Did she hear
what I said? I said that I was *not* doing well. She didn't even ask
me why.

After those experiences, I thought that Americans were actually
insincere. I really believed that they were superficial, as some
French people say. Americans smile and look happy to see you, but
they really don't care about you. It's only for show, for appear-
ances. Americans always seem to smile, even when they are not
happy they smile. I remember some American students in France.
They were always smiling. My friends used to say, "Why do Americans always smile and say 'hello' to strangers?"

The next semester, I didn't see most of my friends and classmates from my first semester. I didn't eat lunch with them in the
cafeteria or the **pizzeria** or study with them in the library anymore.
I saw them around campus occasionally, but they were usually with
new friends. I thought that perhaps Americans easily forget their
old friends. Perhaps they always want *new* friends because they
move often and have to make new friends each time. Having old
friends is like having an old car or an old TV or old clothes. Americans like new things not old things.

I returned to Grenoble in the summer after my first year of college in Chicago. I told my father that I didn't want to continue college in America. I was very embarrassed to tell him because he liked going to college in the United States. He still knew many of his American classmates from college, and they visited each other. My father is very outgoing. He has many friends and likes to socialize. I, on the other hand, like to be by myself more. I like to spend more time reading and studying by myself. We are very different, which is why I didn't tell him of my problems during school in Chicago. I also didn't want to disappoint him. Fortunately, he understood my problems and talked to me for a long time. He talked to me about differences between the Americans and the French. He told me about his first experiences at an American college. He told me that everyone says the Americans and the French are very similar because they were great **allies** in history, the colors on their flags are the same, and they enjoy vacationing in each other's countries. But in fact, he said, American and French cultures are actually quite different.

That was my first year in college. Now I'm in my senior year, and I have many American friends. It has taken me several years, though, to learn about Americans. I think it was difficult for me to make friends at first because my English was not perfect. College students use a lot of slang that I didn't understand at first. I also expected that Americans would be the same as the French, so I was surprised and put off when they weren't.

I think Americans are adventurous. Many of them like to move around and try new things. In America, it's easy to move to another school, or another job, or another place to live, or even to another state. Such movement is not as easy in France. In a word, variety is what Americans like.

I also think they're gregarious. They often have many friends, and those friends may be very different from one another. They may have friends from work, friends from school, friends of the family, friends from hobbies or sports, and friends of friends. My theory is that Americans care about quantity—how much there is of something. The French, however, are more concerned with quality—how good something is. American food proves my theory. The **portions** are large, but sometimes the food is mediocre. But in

allies: friends, especially in war or conflict

portion: amount of food

France, of course, the food is the best, although the portions are usually small.

So, since Americans need more friends, maybe they have less time for each one. To a **newcomer** like me, Americans can seem very superficial at first: friendly on the outside but uncaring on the inside. I realize now that this is probably not true, but you might think this *at first*. You learn a lot about Americans when you go to college here. Most of all, you learn that Americans are really all very different. Eventually, I found that some Americans are exactly like the French and some are completely the opposite.

newcomer:
someone new to a group; a recent arrival

What's the Story About?

Write short answers to these questions. Try to write *more* than one or two words.

1. How long has Thierry been in the United States? _____

   _____

2. Why did Thierry go to college in the United States? _____

   _____

3. How did his father like college in the United States? _____

   _____

4. How does Thierry feel about American food? _____

   _____

5. What did he think of Americans at first? _____

   _____

6. In the end, what does he realize about Americans? _____

   _____

7. What does he mean when he says that Americans are "superficial" and "insincere"? _____

_____

8. What was Thierry's "experiment" with Americans? _____

_____

True or False

Are the following statements about the story true or false? Circle T (true) or F (false).

T   F   1. Thierry's father is from Chicago.

T   F   2. His father always wanted him to go to college in the United States.

T   F   3. Thierry had always believed that American colleges were the best in the world.

T   F   4. With English fluency and a college degree, Thierry will get a good job in the United States.

T   F   5. At first, he hated Chicago.

T   F   6. At first, he thought Americans were very friendly.

T   F   7. The French do not visit each other's homes as much as Americans do.

T   F   8. Thierry's father has "big shoulders" because he eats a lot of pizza.

T   F   9. To Thierry, Americans always seem to be in a rush.

T   F   10. Thierry and his father now have a good relationship.

Guessing Meaning

Guess the correct words from the following list to fill in the blanks. Use the right *form* of each word (verb, noun, adjective, or adverb) and use the right tense of verbs (past, present). The vocabulary comes from the story or the introduction to the story you have just read. However, the sentences are *not* about Thierry's story. Other words in the sentence(s) give you clues to (help you guess) the meaning(s) of the missing word(s).

Verbs	*Nouns*	*Adjectives*	*Adverb*
experiment	perspective	adventurous	occasionally
judge	theory	gregarious	
socialize	well-being	mediocre	
treat		put off	
		sincere	
		superficial	

1. There is a proverb that says, "Never _____ a book by its cover." It means that you cannot form an opinion about something, such as a book, by its appearance alone.

2. Steve had a party last night, but I wasn't invited. I feel _____ by this because I thought we were friends. I'm disappointed, too, because I like to _____ with his friends.

3. How do you _____ your friends? Are you helpful and generous?

4. The army is testing a new weapon. It wants to _____ with less expensive material.

5. My mother calls me once a week to check on me. She's always worried about my _____.

6. There is a _____ about second language learning suggesting that children under age six learn better than adults.

7. Tests and quizzes are useful from the teachers'

    _____, although not necessarily from the students'.

Using the Best Word

Circle the best word to complete each sentence. The vocabulary comes from the story you have just read. However, the sentences are *not* about Thierry's story.

1. Béatrice always asks to help her friends, and when they need her, she does help. She does what she says. She's a *French / insincere / sincere* friend.
2. Tim usually takes the bus to school. *Superficial / Occasionally / Caring*, though, he rides his bike to school.
3. Erin flirts with all the boys in her class. She acts like this to be popular with everyone, not because she actually cares about them. People call her *superficial / sincere / caring*.
4. *Adventurous / Insincere / Gregarious* people like to travel and try new things.
5. Mozart loved parties. He liked to go out socializing frequently. He was quite *well-being / gregarious / genius*.
6. Most good bottles of wine cost over $15.00. For $7.00, you usually get a *superficial / mediocre / unfriendly* or even bad wine.

What Do You Think?

With a classmate or in small groups, discuss the following questions.

1. Look again at the last paragraph of the story. What does Thierry mean when he says Americans can be "friendly on the outside but uncaring on the inside"? Does he think the French are the same? Why or why not?
2. How did you feel about Americans at first? Did you think they were "insincere" and "superficial"? How do you feel now?
3. Imagine that Thierry is in your country. Do you think he would find the people sincere or superficial? Why?

After discussing all of the questions, pick one of them to write about individually. Write your answer in about three paragraphs.

Key Words of the Story

Match the vocabulary words on the left with their meanings on the right. Write the word number on the line next to its meaning. (Dots (•) separate syllables. Stress marks (´) indicate the syllable stressed in pronunciation of the word.)

1. judge (V)

2. per•spec•tive (N)

3. treat (V)

4. sin•cere (Adj)

5. well-be•ing (N)

6. ex•per•i•ment (V)

7. su•per•fi•cial (Adj)

8. oc•ca•sion•al•ly (Adv)

9. so•cial•ize (V)

10. put off (Adj)

11. ad•ven•tur•ous (Adj)

12. gre•gar•i•ous (Adj)

13. the•o•ry (N)

14. me•di•o•cre (Adj)

a. ___ sometimes

b. ___ health or condition

c. ___ to try something in order to learn about it

d. ___ liking action, excitement, change

e. ___ to interact with other people for pleasure

f. ___ average or low quality

g. ___ an idea that has not been proven as fact

h. ___ to form an opinion about value or right and wrong

i. ___ caring and honest in feeling and action

j. ___ discouraged; rejected

k. ___ view; way of looking at something

l. ___ enjoy socializing with many people

m. ___ to act or behave toward someone

n. ___ concerned only with surface or appearance; not sincere

Derived Forms

The table shows some vocabulary from chapter 10. Fill in the different forms of each word in the blank boxes. You can use an English-English (not a bilingual) dictionary. See page 9 in chapter 1 for more explanation.

Verb	Noun	Adjective	Adverb
———			sincerely
	judgment		
occasion			
theorize			
———	superficiality		
		sociable	
			experimentally

Chapter 11

The Awful Misunderstanding

Before You Read the Story

Knowing English is only one consideration when living in the United States. Song, from South Korea, realizes that he has to learn about the people and culture of this country, too. He especially needs to know how men and women treat each other. The way men and women interact in the United States is different from how they interact in Korea. Look carefully at the drawings with the story on the following pages. Can you "read" the story in these drawings?

• • • • • • • • • • • • • • • •

The Awful Misunderstanding

When I lived in Korea, I thought I knew a lot about Americans. I studied American English, watched American television programs, and saw many Americans, especially soldiers, who lived there. But I never studied American behavior. I learned about their food and holidays and so on but not about the interactions between men and women. I assumed that it was the same as in Korea. When I came to the United States, however, I realized that I didn't know very much about how American men and women behave toward each other. I soon learned an embarrassing lesson, one that I will never forget. But now I can say that I *really* know Americans.

I came to the U.S. as a **graduate** student in economics. The university I attended was well known and respected. I was honored

graduate:
studying for a
master's or doctoral
degree

to attend. I studied all the time. My classmates studied a lot, too. The program was very demanding. So the only place I could meet people was in classes, in the cafeteria, in the library, etc. I thought I could find an American girlfriend in class.

I had always been attracted to American women in Korea. I guess I had watched too many American movies. I knew one American student in Korea, but my parents, who are **traditional** and conservative Koreans, would never have accepted a relationship between me and an American woman. I was particularly attracted to **blondes**, and I soon discovered that there were many in America. I never saw blondes in Korea. I became very attracted to them here.

In the U.S., away from my parents, I could date whomever I wanted. In my classes there were some very pretty women. Sometimes one of my classes was boring because the professor would explain things to the class that I already knew. During these times I gazed at some of the female students, in particular at a blond student named Erika. When I looked at Erika, I couldn't hear anything the professor was saying. I was **mesmerized**. I was in love. I tried to sit next to her in class and asked her several times

traditional: preferring old, established customs and beliefs

blondes: people who have blond (yellowish) hair

mesmerized: to be so interested by something or someone that you are not aware of anything else happening around you at that moment

to study with me. I thought I could help her with studying since the class was easy for me.

Erika seemed upset when she noticed me looking at her or when I sat next to her. She would move a couple of desks away from me, but I didn't know why. After class one day I asked Erika about the rings on her fingers. "Are you married?" I asked her. She said, "No! And it's **none of your business** anyway." Why was she so rude to me? Americans were generally very friendly.

Then my troubles began. One of my professors called me up at home and asked me to come see him in his office. The next day I met with him. He told me that some of the female students in his class had complained about me. They said I was "harassing" them. They didn't like the way I looked at them or talked to them sometimes. And the professor agreed with the women. He thought that I must have been harassing them and disrupting the class for them. He told me that I couldn't talk to these women in class and that he had to discuss my behavior with the director of the graduate program.

I was shocked. I told my professor that I had never hurt these women; in fact, I liked them. I told him that they must be mistaken

none of your business: doesn't personally concern you (the question is too personal)

or crazy. Did he think I had done anything wrong? Was he crazy too? After all, he thought I was a brilliant student. I asked him what the punishment would be. He said there would be no punishment, but that I should not talk to them or "harass" them anymore.

I felt so bad about what had happened that I cried when I left the professor's office. I felt so ashamed that I couldn't face the class or the professor again. I didn't go to classes for the rest of the week. I wanted to go back home, to where I understood the people and knew how to behave. On Saturday, I started packing my things to return to Korea.

Complete the Story

What do you think happened to Song? What did he do about his problem? Did he go back to Korea or did he stay in graduate school?

1. Choose a partner in class.
2. With this partner, discuss what Song should do or might do.

3. Write an ending for the story with your partner *or* describe your possible ending to the rest of the class.

What's the Story About?

(Before doing these exercises, read the ending of Song's story at the *end of this chapter.*) Write short answers to these questions. Try to write *more* than one or two words.

1. What is Song's occupation? _____

   _____

2. Why did he come to the United States? _____

   _____

3. Do you think he likes the United States? _____

   _____

4. How does he feel about his parents? _____

   _____

5. What trouble does he have? _____

_____

6. Who is Erika? _____

_____

7. Who helps him with his trouble? _____

_____

8. Song says that he couldn't "face" his classmates again. What does this mean, and why couldn't he face them? _____

_____

True or False

Are the following statements about the story true or false? Circle **T** (true) or **F** (false).

T   F   1. Song went to graduate school to study English.

T   F   2. At first, Song didn't know very much about relations between men and women in the United States.

T   F   3. Song had many American friends, and he socialized frequently.

T   F   4. Song was too conservative to date an American woman.

T   F   5. Erika was mesmerized by Song in class.

T   F   6. His professor thought Song was a brilliant student.

T   F   7. Erika didn't like to sit close to Song.

T   F   8. Song's English tutor told him that he wasn't wrong to be unfamiliar with American expectations.

Guessing Meaning

Guess the correct words from the following list to fill in the blanks. Use the right *form* of each word (verb, noun, adjective, or adverb) and use the right tense of verbs (past, present). The vocabulary comes from the story or the introduction to the story you have just read. However, the sentences are *not* about Song's story. Other words in the sentence(s) give you clues to (help you guess) the meaning(s) of the missing word(s).

Verb	*Nouns*	*Adjectives*	*Adverbs*
accuse	consideration	ashamed	particularly
assume	punishment	brilliant	(or in particular)
complain		demanding	
disrupt		honored	
face		mistaken	
gaze			
harass			
intend			

1. As I sat in the park, I _____ at the ducks in the pond.

2. Some kids in the neighborhood are _____ our dog. They stand by the fence and throw things at the dog. I think I'm going to _____ to their parents. I think that they deserve some _____ for their behavior.

3. The cost of tuition is an important _____ when deciding on a college to attend.

4. The student _____ the class by arguing with the teacher.

5. Every person _____ of a crime in the United States can _____ his or her accuser.

6. In 1989, President George Bush of the United States and President François Mitterand of France gave speeches at the Boston
University graduation. Boston University students,

_____ the graduating seniors, were

_____ by the presence of these statesmen.

Using the Best Word

Circle the best word to complete each sentence. The vocabulary
comes from the story you have just read. However, the sentences are
not about Song's story.

1. When John wears his blue suit, the women in his office think he's
very handsome. They are *attracted / attractive / rude* to him.
2. When Tom first arrived in Japan to teach English, he was unfamiliar with Japanese culture. He *complained / assumed / accuse* that
the language was the biggest difference, not the culture. He was
mistaken / honored / brilliant. Later, when he learned how to act
more like the Japanese, he felt *ashamed / upset / mistaken* of how
he had acted when he first arrived.
3. Many people consider Harvard to be one of the best universities
in the world. The study there is very *brilliant / demanding /
demand* and some of the students are *brilliant / attracted to /
faced*.
4. "Oh, sorry! I didn't *disrupt / face / intend* to miss your party. I
must have forgotten that it was last Saturday."

What Do You Think?

With a classmate or in small groups, discuss the following questions.

1. Why did the female students think that Song was "harassing"
them?

2. Why did Song think that he did nothing wrong, that he didn't hurt the female students at all?

3. Who do you think knew Song better, his English teacher or his economics professor? Explain.

offend: to insult

4. Imagine that some American students in your class accuse you of offensive behavior. Imagine that you, like Song, don't feel you've done anything wrong. What could be **offending** them? What would you do?

5. Imagine that an American woman goes to your country to study. Do you think that your countrymen might "harass" her? That is, would *she* think this way?

After discussing all of the questions, pick one of them to write about individually. Write your answer in about three paragraphs.

Key Words of the Story

Match the vocabulary words on the left with their meanings on the right. Write the word number on the line next to its meaning. (Dots (•) separate syllables. Stress marks (´) indicate the syllable stressed in pronunciation of the word.)

1. con•síd•er•ation (N)

2. as•súme (V)

3. hón•ored (Adj)

4. de•mánd•ing (Adj)

5. at•tráct•ed (Adj)

6. par•tíc•u•lar•ly (Adv)

7. gaze (V)

8. com•pláin (V)

9. ha•ráss (V)

10. dis•rúpt (V)

11. mis• ták•en (Adj)

12. bríl•liant (Adj)

13. pún•ish•ment (N)

14. a•shámed (Adj)

15. face (V)

16. ac•cúse (V)

17. in•ténd (V)

a. ___ to look at steadily, with attention

b. ___ to confront; to see and talk to someone

c. ___ to express pain or what you don't like

d. ___ to believe as true without knowing

e. ___ to bother or irritate repeatedly

f. ___ something to think about or consider

g. ___ difficult; challenging; tough; hard

h. ___ especially; more than others

i. ___ to interrupt and put into disorder

j. ___ grateful; thankful

k. ___ interested in or like

l. ___ penalty for doing wrong

m. ___ unusually intelligent

n. ___ to plan or mean to do

o. ___ to say or claim that someone has done something wrong

p. ___ feeling shame or guilt; disgust with oneself

q. ___ wrong; incorrect

Derived Forms

The table shows some vocabulary from chapter 11. Fill in the different forms of each word in the blank boxes. You can use an English-English (not a bilingual) dictionary. See page 9 in chapter 1 for more explanation.

Verb	Noun	Adjective	Adverb
	assumption		
	complaint	————	
			disruptively
		intentional	
		considerate	
demand			
mistake			

• • • • • • • • • • • • • • •

The End of Song's Story

Then my English writing tutor came to visit me at my apartment. We had a tutoring lesson every Saturday morning. I forgot about our lesson that day because I was upset. When I saw her at the door I thought that she had come to accuse me of something too. She was a woman, after all. Instead, she greeted me in Korean. No American ever did this with me. We had spoken often about my writing and my research papers, and I felt that we had become friends. She had taught English in Korea and Taiwan and knew a lot about my country.

withdraw from:
to remove oneself
voluntarily; to leave

She came in, and I told her right away about leaving. She was shocked. She wanted to talk to me about why I was **withdrawing from** school. She explained how difficult it was to understand the behavior of another culture. She told me that when she first arrived in Korea, people thought that she was rude because she used to say "No" in Korean when she didn't want or like something. "No" is considered rude in Korea, but it's perfectly acceptable in English because English is a very "direct" language. You say what you think.

Likewise, according to my culture, I had done nothing wrong with my classmates. What I had done was no different from what my tutor had done in Korea. I was as unfamiliar with American culture as she was unfamiliar with Korean culture.

The next week, my English tutor explained the misunderstanding to my economics professor and to the female students. They learned a little about Korean culture and understood that I was not an evil person and that I did not intend to harass them. Although I was still very embarrassed, I returned to class. I think my English tutor is the kindest person I have ever known. I am very thankful to her. She taught me about much more than language.

Chapter 12
Out of Africa

Before You Read the Story

Ashford, from Kenya, thought he knew how people would treat him in the United States. He thought white people might treat him differently because he was black. He never thought they would treat him better because he *wasn't* American. Look carefully at the drawings with the story on the following pages. Can you "read" the story in these drawings?

Note to teacher: Please see the remarks in the Preface about stereotypes before doing this chapter. This story is based on an actual incident and was corroborated by other Nigerian and Kenyan students who had comparable experiences. It frankly discusses issues of race that *may*, in unusual circumstances I think, make some teachers or students uncomfortable. Otherwise, it should arouse lively, *honest* discussion. Consider the readiness of your own class before broaching the mature topic of this story.

• • • • • • • • • • • • • • • •

Out of Africa

States: the United States

late teens: about 17 to 19 years of age

late twenties: about 27 to 29 years of age

My brother, Charles, and I moved to the **States** several years ago. He was in his **late teens** and I was in my **late twenties**. We left Kenya because there were few opportunities there for men like us to make money. In Kenya, we worked on our family's farm. It was a good life because we enjoyed working outdoors in the fresh air, but our life would probably never have changed in Kenya. We wanted more out of life than farming.

We decided that in America we would work in business or finance, not farming. It was sad leaving home. We consoled ourselves with the thought that one day, after we had made enough money, we might return to Kenya. In the meantime, we planned to send money back to our **relatives** in Kenya.

We moved to Cambridge, Massachusetts, and stayed with an older Kenyan friend and his family. I found a job in a bank, while my brother attended college full time. After a few months, we were very comfortable and happy with our new lives.

I liked working at the bank. I started out in customer service and then moved to the accounting department after about a year. I made many friends at the bank, and we often went out for **drinks** after work. One of the senior managers at the bank was Kenyan, so we became friends right away. In the summer, the bank formed softball and volleyball teams, and we played other banks. I was having a great time, getting paid well, saving money, and putting Charles through college.

Charles was also content. He liked college and studied all the time. He was a serious student; in fact, he got almost all A's. In

relatives: family members

drinks: here, alcoholic beverages

internship: a student getting practical, professional experience in a job

made up of: composed of

melting pot: The United States is a place where different cultures combine to become more like one (assimilation) and where different races of people mix (although not completely).

fit in: to belong; to be accepted by others

race: here, human group (such as white, black, Asian, etc.)

get along: to be friendly toward each other; to live in harmony

African American: a black American (generally, someone with African family roots)

his second year of studies, he found an **internship** at a bank. With this internship, he earned money to pay his college tuition and would have a good job after graduation.

It seemed that we had made the right decision in leaving Kenya. I had always believed that America was the ideal society, where anyone could succeed with hard work, where anyone could make money. And Charles and I were hard workers. Since American culture was **made up of** many of the world's cultures, a "**melting pot**," we also thought that anybody could **fit in**. But soon I realized how the different **races** and cultures got along in America. Many separate cultures coexist, sometimes not peacefully. Of course, from my study of history I knew that black and white people in America did not always **get along** well.

After living and working in Cambridge for several months, I noticed that people treated me differently because I was from Kenya, but not in a way I had expected. I was not aware of this difference until there was a company party. At the party, there were about one hundred people. Almost all of the **African Americans** were talking and sitting together on one side of the room.

Indians: people from the subcontinent of India (the native, or original, people of America are called "Native Americans," although they were also called "Indians" in the past)

African: someone, like Ashford or Charles, who was born in a country on the African continent, such as Kenya or Nigeria

break down: to experience problems and stop working

lot: area where cars park

jump start: use of the battery of one car to help start another car whose battery is weak

colony: a region controlled by a distant country

There were mostly whites working at the bank, but there were some Asians, **Indians**, and blacks from the Caribbean and Africa, too. They mingled throughout the crowd. I enjoyed mingling, especially with employees that I did not regularly see. At that moment, I realized that I must be different from African Americans.

I had many white, **African**, Caribbean, and Asian friends at the bank but no African American friends. I did not plan it this way; it simply happened without my knowing it. I started to think more and more about African Americans and Africans. I noticed that, in a store for example, the sales clerk was friendlier to me and spent more time with me after he or she realized that I was a foreigner and not American, in particular, not an African American.

Another time, my car **broke down** in the parking **lot** of a store. My battery was dead, and I needed a **jump start**. I had to ask someone for help. I approached a man and a woman in a car, but they drove away from me. I approached a middle-aged white woman who was putting bags into the trunk of her car. She looked frightened—or very concerned—as I walked toward her. When I started to talk to her and ask for help, she became relaxed. She no longer looked scared. We talked for a few minutes, then she asked, "Where are you from?" I told her Kenya, and she said, "Oh, that's very interesting. I'd like to go to Kenya someday. They have those wonderful wild animal parks." (Kenya is famous for its parks, or "game reserves," where elephants, lions, zebras, etc., roam.) She wasn't able to jump-start my car, but she did use her cellular phone to call for someone else to help me. She was very kind; in fact, I think she was flirting with me a little.

These people and others that I met, mostly whites, sometimes seemed relieved or more helpful when they found out that I was not an African American but Kenyan. Since Kenya was once a British **colony**, I speak English with a British accent. Many of my teachers in school in Kenya were British or had learned British English. So people assumed that I was British. When I said I was from Kenya, they seemed very interested in me and my country, like the woman in the parking lot. Whites in particular became friendlier toward me, more willing to help me or talk to me. They also seemed to trust me more than they trusted African Americans.

I found this treatment confusing. I had thought that some Americans would resent foreigners and immigration. There are people in all countries of the world that do not like foreigners or immigrants. They don't like people coming to their country to have what they have. I expected this sort of people to resent me for being *foreign*. However, I didn't meet anyone who resented me for being foreign. Of course, my community had many immigrants.

Soon I began to see myself as being very different from African Americans. I didn't think that we had very much in common. I began to treat them the way some whites did, with caution and reserve. After all, I worked at a bank with mostly whites and other recent African and Caribbean immigrants. I felt I had more in common with them than with African Americans, with whom I interacted less often. I think I even began to feel the subtle prejudices held by some American whites toward African Americans. Some African Americans expected me to act like them or think like them because I was black. Some whites expected me to act British because I was from Kenya. It felt as if people were competing for my loyalty. These differing expectations were very confusing to me. I didn't choose friends for the color of their skin, and I didn't want others to choose me or reject me because of the color of my skin.

I have learned that race relations in America are very complex. Sometimes there's **harmony**, sometimes trouble. Many blacks and whites try to treat each other in a friendly and respectful manner. There are **interracial** couples, for example. Many whites have some black friends, and many blacks have some white friends, especially if they work or go to school together. But there are still tensions and problems between blacks and whites.

Charles never understood my confusion. He hasn't experienced the same differing expectations. He thinks that everyone treated him as a black, and sometimes that meant negatively. The college he attended had a large number of African Americans. Most of his friends, including his girlfriend, have been African Americans. He says that it's difficult to have many white friends. I think perhaps he has **assimilated** into the culture of African Americans and forgotten that he is Kenyan.

I am ten years older than my brother Charles. Maybe our age difference is the reason for our difference in perception. I think of myself as Kenyan; he thinks of himself as black. In America, I think it's possible to forget who you are. I want to stay in America, but I also still want to be Kenyan.

harmony: peace, cooperation between groups

interracial: being of different races (e.g., one African American, one white)

assimilate: to become similar to another cultural group

What's the Story About?

Write short answers to these questions. Try to write *more* than one or two words.

1. Where are Ashford and Charles from and where did they move to? _____

   _____

2. Why did they move? _____

   _____

3. What did they do when they arrived there? _____

   _____

4. How did Ashford feel about America before leaving Kenya? ____

_____

5. How did Ashford expect Americans would treat him? _____

_____

6. Who are Ashford's friends? Who are Charles's friends? _____

_____

7. Why did people like or become more interested in Ashford? ____

_____

8. How did Ashford feel about African Americans? _____

_____

True or False

Are the following statements about the story true or false? Circle T (true) or F (false).

T F 1. When Ashford and his brother moved here, they were teenagers.

T F 2. Ashford's brother was happy to leave Kenya.

T F 3. While Ashford worked in a bank, his brother attended college.

T F 4. Ashford was the only black person at the bank.

T F 5. Ashford and his brother were very content with their new lives.

T F 6. Americans resented Ashford because he was an immigrant.

T F 7. Ashford and his brother are British.

T F 8. Ashford seems to **identify with** whites, while his brother seems to identify with American blacks.

T F 9. Charles didn't like foreigners or immigrants.

T F 10. In the parking lot of a store, Ashford didn't see an elephant getting into the trunk of a car.

identify with: to have experiences and feelings similar to those of someone else

Guessing Meaning

Guess the correct words from the following list to fill in the blanks.
Use the right *form* of each word (verb, noun, adjective, adverb) and
use the right tense of verbs (past, present). The vocabulary comes
from the story you have just read. However, the sentences are *not*
about Ashford's story. Other words in the sentence(s) give you clues to
(help you guess) the meaning(s) of the missing word(s).

Verbs	*Nouns*	*Adjectives*	*Adverb*
coexist	loyalty	content	peacefully
console	perception	famous	
find out	prejudice	ideal	
reject	tension	subtle	
resent	treatment		
trust			

1. The athlete didn't win an Olympic gold medal, but she

   _____ herself with a silver medal. The silver medal was

   still something to be proud of.

2. People that live in cities, "urbanites," often treat strangers with

   caution and reserve at first. They don't _____ them right

   away because that could be dangerous.

3. Before the war in Yugoslavia, many different ethnic groups there

   _____ peacefully.

4. I need to _____ _____ what time the next train

   leaves. If I don't, I won't know what time to get to the train

   station.

5. Martin Luther King Jr. had a dream that one day people would

   not be judged by the color of their skin. He dreamed of an end to _____. Unfortunately, there was much

_____ between blacks and whites during his life-

time.

6. My publisher _____ my idea for a book. She said
that people probably wouldn't buy it.

7. Gary always votes for Democratic candidates. He has a strong

_____ to the Democratic Party.

Using the Best Word

Circle the best word to complete each sentence. The vocabulary
comes from the story you have just read. However, the sentences are
not about Ashford's story.

1. Bill is *gladdened / content / ideal* with his new job. He earns as
   much money as he needs and finds the work interesting. His wife
   thinks he has the *complicated / ideal / peacefully* job and could
   never find a better one.
2. Paul can't tell his girlfriend that she has bad breath because he
   doesn't want to hurt her feelings. Instead, he gives *complicated /
   especially / subtle* hints to her, such as giving her breath mints.
3. Although America invaded Quebec in 1775 (and lost), Canada and
   the United States now coexist *peacefully / especially / eventually*
   as neighbors.
4. Some people think that we spend too much money on the military.
   They *resent / rejected / trust* paying taxes for this.
5. I asked Rachel for her *ideal / treatment / perception* of the problem. I knew that she would probably take a different view than I.
6. When we first moved here, our neighbors were very rude to us.
   We didn't understand this *treatment / harmony / assimilation*
   because we had done nothing wrong.
7. New Orleans, Louisiana, is *ideal / content / famous* for its Cajun-
   style food. Everyone in the country knows about it.

What Do You Think?

With a classmate or in small groups, discuss the following questions.

1. What does Ashford mean when he says, "It felt as if people were competing for my loyalty"?
2. Ashford felt that he had to choose between two groups in America, whites and blacks. Did he make a choice? If so, do you think it was the right choice? Imagine that you were Ashford. What would you have done differently?
3. When you first came to the United States, what did you think of race relations here? How does this compare with race relations in your country?

After discussing all of the questions, pick one of them to write about individually. Write your answer in about three paragraphs.

Key Words of the Story

Match the vocabulary words on the left with their meanings on the right. Write the word number on the line next to its meaning. (Dots (•) separate syllables. Stress marks (´) indicate the syllable stressed in pronunciation of the word.)

1. con•sóle (V)

2. con•tént (Adj)

3. i•dé•al (Adj)

4. có•ex•ist (V)

5. péace•ful•ly (Adv)

6. fá•mous (Adj)

7. find out (V)

8. trust (V)

9. tréat•ment (N)

10. re•sént (V)

11. súb•tle (Adj)

12. préj•u•dice (N)

13. lóy•al•ty (N)

14. re•jéct (V)

15. tén•sion (N)

16. per•cép•tion (N)

a. ___ to believe in without fear

b. ___ stress or hostility

c. ___ how someone is treated

d. ___ the quality of serving or staying with something; fidelity; faithfulness

e. ___ here, a negative opinion based on one's race, ethnicity, religion, or other identification

f. ___ to not accept

g. ___ satisfied

h. ___ the best; perfect

i. ___ to lessen a sense of loss or grief; to comfort

j. ___ to feel or express annoyance at

k. ___ without conflict or trouble

l. ___ to learn; to discover

m. ___ well known and popular

n. ___ delicate; not obvious

o. ___ observation; one's understanding of something

p. ___ to live peacefully with or near each other

Derived Forms

The table shows some vocabulary from chapter 12. Fill in the different forms of each word in the blank boxes. You can use an English-English (not a bilingual) dictionary. See page 9 in chapter 1 for more explanation.

Verb	Noun	Adjective	Adverb
	consolation	———	
	trust		
		resentful	
———			ideally
———	loyalty		
reject			
			comfortably

Appendix: Answers to Exercise Questions

Chapter 1.
The American Classroom

What's in the Story?

Japan, behavior, American education, opinions, classroom

Using the Best Word

1. questioned, disrespectful, disagree
2. encourage, opinions, repeat, prepared
3. independent, freedom
4. critique
5. shocking, comfortable
6. nap, rude
7. pleased
8. control

Key Words of the Story

a.	3	i.	13
b.	5	j.	7
c.	9	k.	6
d.	12	l.	15
e.	11	m.	8
f.	10	n.	16
g.	4	o.	2
h.	14	p.	1

Chapter 2.
The Escalator

What's in the Story?

feeling afraid, screams, Vietnam, escalator, feeling foolish, family

Guessing Meaning

1. had to
2. embarrassing, foolish, scared (or afraid)
3. realized, brave
4. screamed, crawled
5. panic, escape
6. relieved
7. gentle, drowned out
8. impatient
9. grabbed
10. prepared

Key Words of the Story

a.	8	j.	4
b.	17	k.	6
c.	7	l.	14
d.	5	m.	16
e.	15	n.	3
f.	2	o.	9
g.	1	p.	10
h.	13	q.	11
i.	12		

Chapter 3.
The Core of the "Big Apple"

What's in the Story?

disappointment, New York, subway, movies and television, dangerous places, exploring a place

Guessing Meaning

1. dreamed, chance
2. disappointed
3. expectation, wonderful
4. real, realistic, exactly
5. favorite, elegant
6. explored, discovered
7. exciting
8. dangerous, cautious
9. approach, begged
10. incessantly, pedestrians, crowded
11. reveal

Key Words of the Story

a.	7	l.	16
b.	5	m.	9
c.	4	n.	11
d.	3	o.	8
e.	6	p.	10
f.	2	q.	13
g.	1	r.	19
h.	17	s.	18
i.	15	t.	22
j.	12	u.	20
k.	14	v.	21

Chapter 4.
Back to School

What's in the Story?

medicine, Jewish, discussions, Russia, ESL classes, adult student

True or False

1.	F	5.	F
2.	F	6.	F
3.	T	7.	T
4.	F	8.	F

Guessing Meaning

1. registered
2. shares
3. tragic
4. surprised, kid
5. argued, smart, boring
6. activity, worried
7. memorize, pairs
8. confusing, waste, nightmare

Key Words of the Story

a.	11	i.	8
b.	9	j.	12
c.	15	k.	7
d.	14	l.	4
e.	13	m.	3
f.	6	n.	1
g.	10	o.	2
h.	5		

Chapter 5.
"Anything Else with That?"

True or False

1.	F	6.	T
2.	F	7.	T
3.	T	8.	F
4.	F	9.	F
5.	T	10.	T

Guessing Meaning

1. stared
2. fluently, get by, practiced
3. nervous
4. common, expression

5. turn, ordered
6. are in a hurry
7. flirts
8. helpless
9. noise
10. splashed, soaked
11. popular, skip

Key Words of the Story

a.	2	j.	4
b.	15	k.	10
c.	3	l.	11
d.	16	m.	5
e.	1	n.	7
f.	17	o.	9
g.	14	p.	6
h.	13	q.	8
i.	12		

Chapter 6.
"For Here or To Go?"

True or False

1.	F	5.	F
2.	T	6.	F
3.	F	7.	F
4.	T	8.	T

Guessing Meaning

1. pointed, made
2. remind
3. free time, busy
4. phrases, trouble, slang
5. opportunity, upset
6. at ease
7. couple
8. missed
9. piles
10. right away, starve

Key Words of the Story

a.	5	i.	1
b.	4	j.	8
c.	6	k.	9
d.	3	l.	10
e.	15	m.	14
f.	16	n.	13
g.	7	o.	12
h.	2	p.	11

Chapter 7.
"I'll Say What I Want"

True or False

1.	T	5.	F
2.	F	6.	F
3.	T	7.	F
4.	T	8.	T

Guessing Meaning

1. talkative, outgoing, express, cute
2. intensive
3. annoyed, react, frustrated
4. campus
5. conservative, interaction, restrictions
6. are supposed to, are used to

Key Words of the Story

a.	3	h.	11
b.	13	i.	12
c.	14	j.	1
d.	7	k.	2
e.	8	l.	5
f.	9	m.	6
g.	10	n.	4

Chapter 8.
Time to Relax

True or False

1.	T	6.	F
2.	F	7.	T
3.	T	8.	T
4.	F	9.	F
5.	T	10.	T

Guessing Meaning

1. linger, rush
2. rarely, leisurely
3. peculiar, habit
4. stressed out
5. obey
6. obsessed
7. relax, accomplished
8. take [your] time
9. related to
10. attend

Key Words of the Story

a.	5	i.	4
b.	6	j.	3
c.	15	k.	11
d.	14	l.	10
e.	7	m.	2
f.	13	n.	9
g.	8	o.	1
h.	12		

Chapter 9.
Our Parents' Goals

Using the Best Word

1. frivolous
2. pressured
3. variety
4. achieved
5. depressed
6. tolerate, view
7. familiar
8. sacrifices, set
9. excel at, compete
10. fail

Key Words of the Story

a.	11	h.	8
b.	3	i.	7
c.	12	j.	13
d.	1	k.	9
e.	4	l.	5
f.	10	m.	6
g.	2		

Chapter 10.
Like Having an Old Car

True or False

1.	F	6.	T
2.	T	7.	T
3.	F	8.	F
4.	F	9.	T
5.	F	10.	T

Guessing Meaning

1. judge
2. put off, socialize
3. treat
4. experiment
5. well-being
6. theory
7. perspective

Using the Best Word

1. sincere
2. Occasionally
3. superficial
4. Adventurous
5. gregarious
6. mediocre

Key Words of the Story

a.	8	e.	9
b.	5	f.	14
c.	6	g.	13
d.	11	h.	1

i. 4   l. 12
j. 10   m. 3
k. 2   n. 7

Chapter 11.
The Awful Misunderstanding

True or False

1. F   5. F
2. T   6. T
3. F   7. T
4. F   8. T

Guessing Meaning

1. gazed
2. harassing, complain, punishment
3. consideration
4. disrupted
5. accused, face
6. particularly, honored

Using the Best Word

1. attracted
2. assumed, mistaken, ashamed
3. demanding, brilliant
4. intend

Key Words of the Story

a. 7   j. 3
b. 15   k. 5
c. 8   l. 13
d. 2   m. 12
e. 9   n. 17
f. 1   o. 16
g. 4   p. 14
h. 6   q. 11
i. 10

Chapter 12.
Out of Africa

True or False

1. F   6. F
2. F   7. F
3. T   8. T
4. F   9. F
5. T   10. T

Guessing Meaning

1. consoled
2. trust
3. coexisted
4. find out
5. prejudice, tension
6. rejected
7. loyalty

Using the Best Word

1. content, ideal
2. subtle
3. peacefully
4. resent
5. perception
6. treatment
7. famous

Key Words of the Story

a. 8   i. 1
b. 15   j. 10
c. 9   k. 5
d. 13   l. 7
e. 12   m. 6
f. 14   n. 11
g. 2   o. 16
h. 3   p. 4